THE PIMERÍA ALTA

Missions & More

JAMES E. OFFICER

MARDITH SCHUETZ–MILLER

BERNARD L. FONTANA

Editors

THE SOUTHWESTERN MISSION RESEARCH CENTER

TUCSON, ARIZONA

ISBN 0-915076-13-6
First Edition

Compiled and coordinated by James E. Officer and Bernard Fontana
Edited by Sandra Scott
Designed by Christina Watkins
Typography and production by Penny Smith, TypeWorks
Printed by Thomson-Shore, Inc.

Institutional Credits
    Arizona State Museum: pages 45, 91 (#30362), 92, 93, and 96
    (#37089). Arizona Historical Society: pages 38 (Calabazas), 41,
    and 46. D'Anville Collection, Bibliotheque Nationale, Paris,
    France: pages 36–37. National Park Service, Western
    Archeological and Conservation Center: pages 10, 12, 67, 69,
    76, 84, 88, and 90. Smithsonian Institution: pages 18, 19, 22,
    23, 24, 45, 73, and 81.

Frontispiece: The village of Arizpe, Sonora, 1957. *James Officer*

IN
MEMORY OF

JAMES E. OFFICER

1924–1996

Un Verdadero Pimalteño

CONTENTS

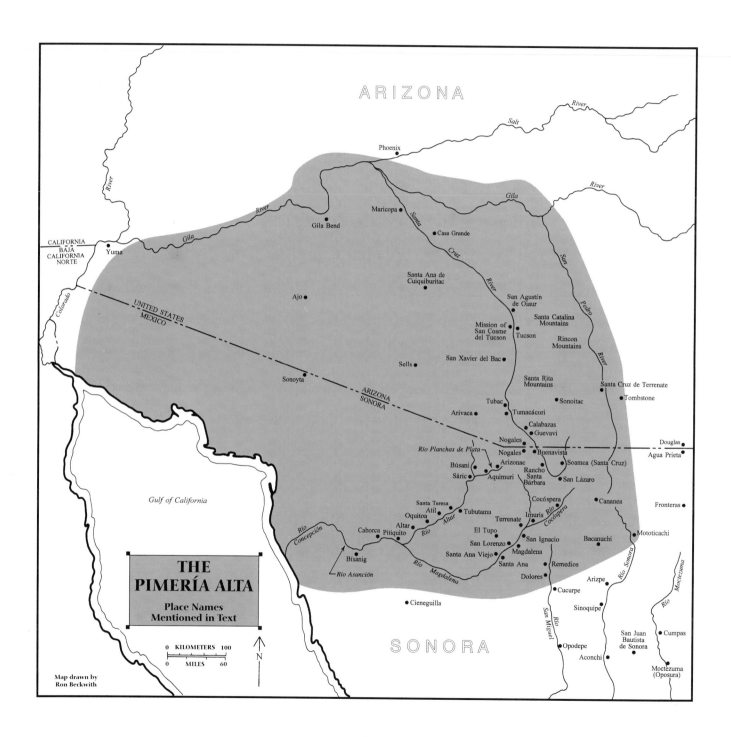

ARIZONA

SONORA

Salt River

River

Gila River

Phoenix

Maricopa

Gila Bend

Santa

Cruz

Gila

San

Pedro

River

CALIFORNIA
BAJA
CALIFORNIA
NORTE

Colorado

River

Yuma

UNITED STATES
MEXICO

Ajo

Santa Ana de
Cuiquiburitac

San Agustín
de Oiaur

Santa Catalina
Mountains

Casa Grande

Sonoyta

ARIZONA
SONORA

Sells

Mission of
San Cosme
del Tucson

Tucson

Rincon
Mountains

San Xavier del Bac

Santa Rita
Mountains

Santa Cruz de Terrenate

Tubac

Sonoitac

Tombstone

Arivaca

Tumacácori

Calabazas

Guevavi

Nogales

Río Planchas de Plata

Nogales

Búsani

Arizonac

Buenavista

Soamca (Santa Cruz)

Douglas

Agua Prieta

Sáric

Aquimuri

Rancho
Santa
Bárbara

San Lázaro

Gulf of California

Santa Teresa

Atil

Tubutama

Oquitoa

Altar

Río

Altar

Cocóspera

Río

Cocóspera

Cananea

Fronteras

Río
Concepción

Caborca

Pitiquito

Terrenate

El Tupo

Imuris

San Lorenzo

San Ignacio

Bacanuchi

Mototicachi

Bisanig

Río Asunción

Río Magdalena

Santa Ana Viejo

Magdalena

Santa Ana

Remedios

Dolores

Río Sonora

Río Moctezuma

Cieneguilla

Cucurpe

Arizpe

Sinoquipe

San Juan
Bautista
de Sonora

Cumpas

San Miguel

Río

Opodepe

Aconchi

Moctezuma
(Oposura)

**THE
PIMERÍA ALTA**

Place Names
Mentioned in Text

0   KILOMETERS   100

0   MILES   60

Map drawn by
Ron Beckwith

N

INTRODUCTION

BY
JAMES E. OFFICER

The inspiration for this volume lies in the visits to Spanish colonial churches in Northwestern Sonora, Mexico which the Southwestern Mission Research Center sponsors each spring and fall. The center (usually referred to simply as SMRC) is a non-profit educational corporation founded in 1965 by a small group of historians and has its headquarters in Tucson. Although the SMRC is not affiliated with any religious organization, its founders gave it the name it bears in recognition of the fact that church records are among the most important documents for reconstructing the early history of Mexico and the American Southwest.

The person who came up with the mission tour idea was Tucsonan Lea Ramírez Ward and, in 1974, she organized the Sonoran trips as a fund-raising endeavor of the League of Mexican American Women and the Tucson Museum of Art League. Two years later, when the leagues turned to other projects, the SMRC began sponsoring the church visits with assistance from Lea, who has been a major factor in their success ever since.

Another important early contributor to that success was Dr. Charles William Polzer, S.J., one of the founders of the SMRC. He was a frequent lecturer on the original tours and continued in that role after the SMRC became responsible for arranging and conducting them.

From the beginning, the focus of the tours has been Northwestern Sonora, an area once inhabited by large numbers of Pima Indians and known to the Spaniards as *La Pimería Alta*, Land of the Upper (or Northern) Pima. In 1687 Father Eusebio Francisco Kino was the first Roman Catholic missionary to undertake conversion of these Indians; and it is owing to this association that people refer to the Sonoran trips as Kino Mission Tours.

Originally, most of the persons traveling on these tours were from Arizona. More recently, they have come from all over the United States and from some foreign countries as well. The trip has been particularly appealing to writers, artists, and photographers, and tour sponsors have benefitted from the publicity such individuals have generated.

One of the earliest tour boosters was free-lance writer Lawrence Cheek. Another was artist Erni Cabat whose travels to Sonora between 1975 and 1981 produced three beautiful booklets filled with color sketches of the Pimería Alta church facades, as well as their main and side altars. Hazel Fontana, wife of one of the contributors to this volume, prepared many pencil drawings of the churches which have been widely circulated as note cards.

Several times representatives of *Sunset* magazine have been aboard our Sonora tour bus and have favored us with beautifully illustrated stories. A television crew from the British Broadcasting Corporation went along on one of the trips during the 1980s and included information about the Kino missions in a series of telecasts related to Mexico and her history.

Income generated through the mission tours has assisted with financing the publication of a number of books concerned with Spanish colonial history in Mexico and the American Southwest. It has also been used to meet certain costs of the Documentary Relations of the Southwest project at the Arizona State Museum and to pay for the travel expenses of individual scholars. Last, but certainly not least, it has aided the people of several Sonoran towns with maintenance and preservation of their Spanish colonial churches. Among the communities benefitting from this assistance have been San Ignacio, Santa Ana Viejo, Oquitoa, and Tubutama.

For many years, those taking the Sonoran trips have received free copies of the *Kino Guide*, a book about the life of Eusebio Francisco Kino and a guide to his missions and monuments. Written by Father Polzer, with excellent maps by the late Don Bufkin, this volume has been of inestimable assistance in providing background on Kino and his work in the Pimería Alta. Regrettably, the *Kino Guide* is now out of print and, while Father Polzer plans to prepare a revised and enlarged version, it could well be some time before it becomes available.

During their deliberations early in 1994, members of the SMRC Board of Directors voted to undertake the preparation of a new book that could provide readers with the kind of information included in the *Kino Guide* plus additional data about the Pimería Alta: its geography, history, people, culture and folklore, economy,

Ted and Nancy Johnson on the nature walk near Pitiquito, 1987. Nicholas Bleser

Tour members hear a lecture at Mission Caborca, 1996. Nicholas Bleser

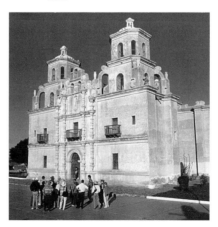

flora and fauna, and its relationship to the remainder of Sonora and to Mexico in general. Board members Mardith Schuetz–Miller, James E. Officer, and Bernard L. Fontana volunteered to serve as editors and to contribute one or more chapters. Others on the board also volunteered or were asked to prepare sections relating to their specialties. In addition, the editors called upon other persons who were not board members, but who had long been SMRC supporters, to help with contributions. The result of the board's action is the volume you now have before you.

The extent and variety of information in these pages may well exceed the interests of average individuals, but all the topics covered here respond to questions that persons visiting the Sonoran missions have asked through the years. More than anything else, the authors have produced a general reference work on the Pimería Alta, and most readers will be pleased to know that one does not have to study it from beginning to end in order to discover and appreciate the plot.

Those who have contributed to this book would like to dedicate it to the late Tom Naylor, whose knowledge and good humor were so important to the Kino Mission Tours as they were maturing; to Marjorie Gould and her late husband Frank, who kept track of all the good folks traveling with us prior to 1992; to Julieta Bustamente Portillo, who has more recently taken on that task; and, finally, to Adán Morales, the best damned bus driver anybody ever rode with.

Left to right: staff member George Malaby, motel and ranch owner José Luis Vanegas, and tour member Charles Luttrell at a mission tour barbecue near Caborca, 1994. Bernard Fontana

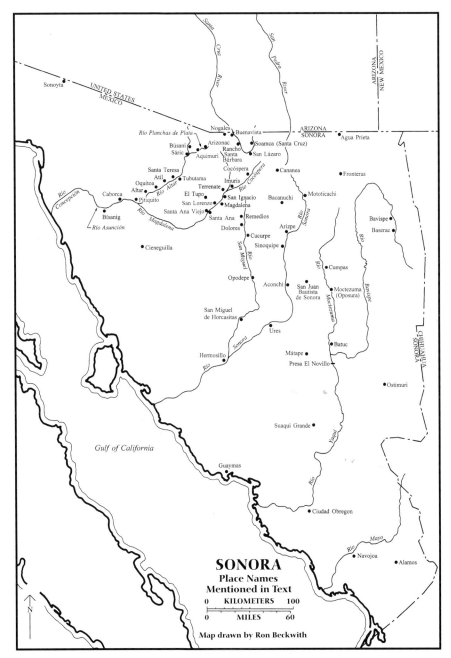

SONORA
Place Names
Mentioned in Text

0 — KILOMETERS — 100
0 — MILES — 60

Map drawn by Ron Beckwith

THE NATURAL SETTING

BY
ROBERTA J. STABEL

La Pimería Alta, arid and rugged, lies within the Sonoran Desert. The typical landscape has wide river valleys surrounded by dramatic, seemingly bare mountains, blue and brooding during the day, reddened in the reflected setting sun. These mountains are the result of faulting and folding that began twenty to twenty-five million years ago, at the same time that the sandstone country of northern Arizona and southern Utah was being lifted to form a high plateau. Valleys between the rough-looking ranges are filled with debris from eons of erosion, thousands of feet thick in places. The mountains seem to be islands rising out of alluvium lakes.

Rainfall amounts vary throughout the Pimería Alta. In general, the lowest precipitation occurs in western Sonora and Arizona where it averages four to ten inches annually, an amount that gradually increases toward the east, away from the dry coastal region, reaching annual averages of ten to sixteen inches.

Sonoran Desert rains occur in two seasons. The summer storms of July through September originate in the Pacific Ocean and come to us from the Gulf of California. The summer storms (*las aguas*) are those that produce the most rain, about five inches annually in the vicinity of Tucson. Typically, the storms are localized and short-lived, but arrive in violent bursts with high winds, lightning, and thunder.

Winter rains originate in the Pacific as well, but largely from off the coast of upper California rather than across the Gulf of California. These quiet, longer-lasting storms cover a larger area and are known regionally as *las equipatas*, a term originating with the Cahitan-speaking people of southern Sonora. While summer rains bring flash floods in arroyos, the winter rains are those that sometimes cause dramatic flooding over wide areas. Of Tucson's twelve-inch total annual average rainfall, slightly more than three inches fall in November through March, December being the wettest month with an inch or so.

Winter temperatures vary considerably. In the low western deserts it seldom freezes, but nighttime freezing is frequent in the higher grasslands and along major rivers. Snow is common at elevations over seven thousand feet and occurs at lower elevations for brief periods during the winter. Temperature inversions are common, and low-lying areas can be from ten to twenty degrees colder than nearby locations a few hundred feet higher. Plant species unable to tolerate freezing are not found along major rivers such as the upper Santa Cruz and San Pedro.

Summertime temperatures peak around the time of the June solstice, and in the lower deserts the average highs are above one hundred degrees Fahrenheit for days at a time. Humidity is low, 5 to 15 percent. The high tempera-

Facing page: **organ pipe and saguaro cacti, Organ Pipe Cactus National Monument.** George A. Grant tures are mitigated by the arrival of the summer rains, usually in late June or early July.

A Dry and Lively Land.

The arid western region of the Pimería Alta is a microphyllus (little-leaved) desert where dominant plants are white bursage, or burro weed, and creosote bush. Some 85 percent of this western region is made up of plains and sloping piedmonts (*bajadas*) of low gradient.

Most of the rest of the Pimería Alta, higher mountain elevations excluded, has crassicaulescent (stem succulent) vegetation and is typified by foothill paloverde, cholla, prickly pear, saguaro, and barrel cactus as well as by mesquite, ironwood, and acacia trees larger than those found along drainageways in the Lower Colorado Valley. Near Pitiquito and Caborca are good stands of columnar cactus—organ pipe, senita, and cardón—in addition to saguaro. This area has five seasons instead of four: spring, foresummer or dry summer, summer monsoon, fall, and winter.

Deeply eroded aprons of debris, washed down from the mountains, slope gradually to the valleys. On these *bajadas*, plant life becomes wonderfully diverse, with large columnar cacti being the most eye catching. The giant saguaro in southern Arizona and northern Sonora, the senita and organ pipe in Sonora and southwestern Arizona, and the huge cardón farther to the south in Sonora need well-drained, gravelly soil. They can tolerate freezing temperatures for only brief periods. Like other cacti their leaves have been reduced to needles and/or glochids—sharp,

Mission Tumacácori and the Santa Rita Mountains.

barbed bristles. Stems are covered by a thick, waxy, photosynthetic skin that performs the food-making function of leaves. During rainy periods they can store water in their stems for use in drier times, and like the root systems of all cacti, theirs are shallow and widespread to take advantage of brief rains. Other common *bajada* cacti include prickly pear, cholla, pin cushion, barrel, and hedgehog.

Additional plants in this community are ironwood, catclaw, hackberry, and foothill paloverde, with associated ground cover plants bursage and brittlebush. Ocotillo, with its long, spiny, whip-like, and usually bare stems, is also abundant. During early spring the stem tips develop plumes of bright orange flowers, and after a warm rain ocotillo will promptly sprout leaves. Its branches often are used in the construction of fences and ramadas.

Watercourses run along the lowest parts of the valleys. Banks of permanent rivers and streams have well-developed communities of cottonwood, willow, walnut, hackberry, catclaw, and mesquite as well as many shrub and grass species, but few cacti. In the washes (*arroyos*), water runs for brief periods after a rain.

It is away from the water-courses in fine-grained soils of the lower valleys that creosote bush grows in abundance, often in almost pure stands. Creosote grows in all four North American deserts, thriving in heat, cold, drought, and in poorly drained and alkaline soils. The large amount of resin in the leaves helps prevent water loss by decreasing the amount of ultraviolet light that can reach the interior of the leaf. Its unpleasant taste guards against its being eaten. Creosote grows either from seeds or, when the center of the plant dies, by clon-

Ironwood tree in bloom on the Papago Indian Reservation, 1980. Bernard Fontana

Organ pipe and saguaro cacti north of Tubutama, 1987. Bernard Fontana

Barrel cactus in bloom. George H. H. Huey

ing, growing outward in a ring. It is one of the more ancient plants, the oldest known to have lived for more than nine thousand years.

In the semi-desert grasslands above the desert are found various species of agave, succulent plants that store large quantities of water in their leaves. They are not cacti though they appear similar. Growing with agave are sotol, yucca, and some species of prickly pear, cholla, and barrel cactus as well as mesquite, paloverde, ocotillo, white thorn and other acacia, mimosa, and many grass species.

Mesquite, acacia, ironwood, netleaf hackberry, and paloverde provide shade for cactus seedlings, and in higher latitudes, shelter from frost. Often called nurse plants, they provide litter that helps nourish seedlings and protects them from being trampled or eaten.

At about 4,000 feet juniper and oak make their appearance, and slightly higher, pinyon trees grow among them. Higher still, above about 6,500 feet, the evergreen forest takes over with familiar western pines, ponderosa being dominant. Douglas fir forests grow at the highest elevations of the higher mountains of southern Arizona—the Santa Catalinas, Rincons, and Santa Ritas. This forest also includes white fir, aspen, and limber pine.

Buckhorn cholla cactus near the Catalina Mountains. George H. H. Huey

Palmer agave. George H. H. Huey

Desert plants use three major tactics to cope with extremes of aridity and heat: 1) Leaves are greatly reduced in size, and in some species appear only during wet periods; 2) Leaves are totally absent, as in cacti; and 3) Leaves, stems, and/or roots store water, enabling plants to last for long periods without rainfall. In fact, these plants will rot in humid environments. Many of these xerophytes, plants that have adapted to extreme dryness, are also halophytes, plants tolerant of large amounts of salt in the soil.

Many plants drop their leaves during dry, hot, or cold periods and become dormant. After a rain, however, they can leaf out rather quickly. Paloverde, with its green bark, can carry on photosynthesis even when leafless. There is so much sunlight in the desert that plants do not have to use it efficiently.

Annual plants (ephemerals) sprout, flower, go to seed, and die, most in early spring, others after the summer rains. Their abundance is related to the amount of winter rainfall. In a good year, the desert floor is carpeted for brief periods with color from blossoms of prickly and Mexican gold poppy, desert zinnia, penstemon, bladderpod, paperdaisy, desert marigold, apricot and globemallow, sand and desert verbena, phacelia, owl's clover, tackstem, and lupine.

Animals have also adapted to the extremes of temperature and rainfall. A few require no water, some get moisture from succulent plants, and others obtain it from the insects and other small animals they eat. Kangaroo rats do not drink water at all but manufacture it from the seeds they eat, thriving in some of the driest desert areas.

Some animals are active only at night, spending days underground. Others have strategies to cope with daytime heat. At midday, birds can be seen ventilating, wings outspread and bills agape; cottontails and ground squirrels lie panting in the shade, sprawled belly-down in freshly dug depressions. The ubiquitous roadrunner is out in the heat of the day, sprinting with mouth open, pausing in the shade of shrubs and fenceposts, grabbing a grasshopper here, a lizard there, getting all the moisture it needs from its food.

The variety of Sonoran Desert habitats allows for many species of snakes, lizards, and amphibians. After the first soaking summer rains leave sizeable puddles, spadefoot toads come from underground, singing lustily in search of mates. By the time the puddles dry up, the toads will have mated, laid their eggs, young will have devel-

oped, and all disappeared again beneath the mud.

Common mammals include coyote, deer, collared peccary (javelina), and coatimundi, a raccoonlike animal found at lower mountain elevations. The confines of the Pimería Alta also feature black-tailed and antelope jackrabbit, desert cottontail, mice, rats, kit fox, gray fox, badger, raccoon, four species of skunk, squirrel, pocket gopher, desert shrew, bat, ringtail cat, bobcat, desert bighorn, mountain lion, pronghorn antelope, and in the higher mountains, black bear and porcupine. The region formerly boasted jaguar, beaver, wild turkey, and parrots. People exterminated grizzly bears and wolves in the southwestern United States and northern Mexico in the early twentieth century.

Desert Sufficiency.

The natural landscape has changed since the arrival of the Spaniards due to livestock grazing, control of wildfire, pumping of underground water, paving of land surfaces, and other interacting factors not well understood, one of which is probably a small change in climate. In former times, streambeds were not cut so deeply as today and running water was closer to the surface, making ditch irrigation more feasible. There

Antelope jackrabbit. Roberta Stabel

The ubiquitous roadrunner.
Roberta Stabel

Western diamondback rattlesnake. George H. H. Huey

15

were more grasses and fewer mesquites and shrubs.

With sufficient soaking rain, the Desert People could plant their seeds of corn, squash, and tepary beans along stream banks and at the fertile mouths of desert washes, and subsequent rains would bring the plants to maturity. Insufficient rain resulted in food scarcity and hunger. In prehistoric times about twenty-five plant species were cultivated. Enormous knowledge was required for efficient utilization of these plants, with intricate complexities of timing and execution.

Even more important to the Desert People's livelihood were gathering wild plants and hunting. Of the more than 2,500 higher plant forms in the Sonoran Desert, more than 425 have edible parts. Mesquite was one of the more important food sources. Efficient in the use of resources and energy, mesquite trees required no human assistance or irrigation, pesticides, or herbicides. People spent a great deal of energy in gathering, grinding, and sifting the pods, however. Nutritious bean pods form and ripen in early summer and again in midsummer. Indians ground the dry, sweet pods into a fine meal that could be mixed with water for a thick mush or with more water to make a refreshing drink. The flour could be layered in a basket, sprinkled with water, and stored as a chunk, later to be broken into pieces and mixed with water. Mesquite's clear sap and sap-blackened bark were used to make black pigment with which to decorate earthenware pottery. Mesquite wood is still used for fuel, building construction, and furniture.

Saguaro fruit matures at the beginning of the rainy season at the end of June or early July, a time when other foods are scare. Its ripening marked the beginning of the O'odham new year, and with it came their most important ceremony, the *náwai't* (from *nawai*, liquor, and *ta*, the suffix which means to make). O'odham drank fermented saguaro fruit syrup as part of the ceremony to "bring down the clouds."

Buds of staghorn cholla, one of the foods ready to eat earliest in the spring, were another important food source. Steamed, boiled, pickled, or dried, a four-ounce serving contains more calcium than a glass of milk. Wolfberries and chiltepines, the small, native hot chiles, contain vitamins A, B_2, and C. Many seeds, such as those of the saguaro, barrel cactus, and devil's claw (*martynia*), are rich in oils containing the B vitamins. Amaranth greens grow during the summer rains and contain calcium, vitamin A, and other vitamins.

O'odham would travel and camp for days to gather and eat Emory oak acorns, which ripen in the late summer, require no processing, and can be eaten from the tree. People also gathered pinyon nuts, various roots, and the banana-shaped fruits of *yucca baccata*.

O'odham preserved foods that kept well, and consumed others on the spot. They roasted the heart of the agave (*mescal*) in pits, many of which can still be found on hillsides. Although few people in Arizona now cook agave hearts, this sweet food can be purchased in Sonoran markets. Using a distillation process introduced by Spaniards, *mescaleros*, or moonshiners, distill a smooth but potent liquor from these hearts in rural towns all over modern Sonora even as they did in colonial times.

People found materials for coiled baskets in cattail flower stalks, yucca leaves and roots, willow, beargrass, and devil's claw, and wove sotol leaves into sleeping mats and sandals or twisted them into cordage.

Creosote bush is probably the most important medicinal plant in all four North American deserts. It is used to treat colds, chest infections, intestinal ailments, cancer, arthritis, dandruff, painful menstruation, and other afflictions. It can be boiled to make tea, steamed as an inhalant, and dried and powdered for a poultice. Its resins are said to contain an antioxidant. The plant is host to an insect larvae whose lac secretions collect on creosote branches. This lacquer was melted and used by O'odham (Pimans) to mend cracks and to plug holes in earthenware vessels.

We often think of the desert as a hostile environment, but for the plants and animals living here it is neither hostile nor benign. It's simply *there*, and many of its dwellers could not survive elsewhere. Until the twentieth century and the advent of modern technology, deserts were thinly populated and people lived lightly upon the land. The resources for food, drink, clothing, medicine,

and shelter are here if one knows where to find them and how to use them. Much of that knowledge is now being forgotten as fewer and fewer people rely on their desert surroundings for subsistence; many of the old gathering and hunting places are no longer accessible or have been converted to other uses; and once-reliable water sources have disappeared because of underground pumping and erosion-causing activities.

As different cultures meet, mingle, and evolve, many of the fine-tuned human technologies of the past fade from memory and view, replaced by other responses to human needs. But the desert lives, let us hope, eternally.

Night blooming cereus. George H. H. Huey

The Santa Cruz River at Tumacacori, summer, 1994. Roberta Stabel

BUREAU OF AMERICAN ETHNOLOGY, U.S. WILLIAM DINWIDDIE, PHOTOGRAPHER.

THE O'ODHAM

BY
BERNARD L. FONTANA

"**O**'odham" in the language of the aboriginal inhabitants of the northern Sonoran Desert means "people." Had there been no O'odham here in the late seventeenth century, there would have been no missionaries and no missions. People who had not yet "heard the good news of Jesus Christ" were the *raison d'être* for Spain's expansion into this area.

Roman Catholic missionaries were not only representatives of the Christian faith, they were also agents of the Spanish Crown; and, at their hands, Indians were expected to become more than practicing Christians. They were also supposed to evolve into God-fearing Spaniards, even if at the lowest status.

Thus, it was neither gold nor glory that initiated Europe's presence in the Pimería Alta. What propelled the Jesuit missionary, Father Eusebio Francisco Kino, to the Rim of Christendom in 1687 was the prospect of new conver-

Facing page: **O'odham woman making flour tortillas, Pitiquito, 1894.** Wm. Dinwiddie

Jose Juan Cristobal, O'odham of San Xavier del Bac, 1894.
Wm. Dinwiddie

sions to the Christian faith and to Spanish vassalage. He also hoped the O'odham would raise livestock to help support a missionary program in Baja California. These aspirations sent him forth on Pimería Alta paths, an enterprise to which he devoted the remaining two dozen years of his life. He died in Sonora in 1711 at the age of sixty-five in the village now formally known as Magdalena de Kino.

A Babel of Labels.

Who were the people among whom Father Kino and his Jesuit and Franciscan successors wished so ardently to fulfill the admonition of John the Baptist, "Make straight in the desert a highway for our God"?

As early as the late sixteenth century Spaniards encountered peoples living in what today are parts of southern Sonora and Chihuahua who spoke mutually intelligible dialects of the same language. Although all these people referred to themselves by dialectical variations of the term *o'odham*, Spaniards unaccountably labelled them with the O'odham term for "nothing," *pimahaitu*. Thus "Pima" became the foreigners' designation for large numbers of men, women, and children who lived in settlements scattered throughout mountains and valleys in southeastern Sonora and today's southwestern Chihuahua.

By the twentieth century, the term "Pima" as used in the United States had come to be restricted to the O'odham living on the Gila and Salt River reservations in southern Arizona. "Piman" came to be the term used by linguists and ethnologists to refer to all peoples speaking dialects of this single language. Thus, in modern usage, "Piman" is equivalent to "O'odham," and both Pimas and Tohono O'odham (Papagos) are Pimans.

When Father Kino, his fellow Jesuits, and Spanish soldiers encountered people living in northern Sonora, they quickly realized the natives spoke dialects of the same language heard farther to the south and were therefore also "Pimas." To avoid confusion, Father Kino referred to them as "*Pimas Altos*" or "Northern Pimas," and to the area where they lived as the "*Pimería Alta*."

Without explanation for their conceptualizations, Spaniards applied still more labels to what seemed to them to be meaningful sub-groups of Northern Pimans. Thus Father Kino wrote of the "*Sobaípuris*" who lived along the San Pedro and Santa Cruz Rivers in southern Arizona; of the "*Pimas*" who lived in communities from his mission headquarters at Dolores on the east to Tubutama on the west as well as on the Gila River; and of the "*Sobas*," the O'odham who lived at Oquitoa, Caborca, and other nearby settlements. Before the eighteenth century was over, Spaniards also referred to various northern O'od-

ham as "*Piatos*" (a contraction of *Pimos Altos*), "*Gileños*" (Gila River residents), and "*Papabi-Ootam.*"

It was a contemporary of Father Kino, a Spanish soldier named Juan Mateo Manje, who introduced the label "*Papabota*" into the literature. (It may derive from the O'odham word for tepary beans, *bá-bawi*, although this is debateable.) The term soon evolved into "*Papago*" and was used primarily to designate the various groups of O'odham living in the riverless desert west of Tucson and east of Ajo, Arizona, a vast tract of land now encompassed by the main body of today's 2,700,000-acre Papago Indian Reservation. After the mid-nineteenth century, when southern Arizona was carved out of northern Mexico via the 1854 Gadsden Purchase, the O'odham living north of the international boundary came to be conceptualized by European Americans as two groups, the Pima and the Papago. The former were residents along the Gila and Salt Rivers and the latter were Pimans residing elsewhere within the territory.

In their adoption of a new tribal constitution in 1986, the qualified voters elected to change their designation from Papago Tribe of Arizona to the Tohono O'odham Nation. *Tohono* is the Piman word for desert; thus,

Tohono O'odham means Desert People. Not wishing any longer to be called Papagos, the members of this group now prefer instead to be called Tohono O'odham, a request generally honored by persons who write or speak about them. Except that the name of the Papago Indian Reservation has not yet been officially changed by the United States Board on Geographic Names, "Papago" is a concept in the United States that belongs to the past rather than to the present or future. In Sonora, however, the word persists as a label.

To distinguish themselves from the Desert People, the Gila and Salt River Pimas now sometimes refer to themselves as the *'akimel o'odham*, the River People, although they remain officially the Pimas.

Three Adaptations.

The cultural realities among the O'odham of the Pimería Alta seem never to have been clearly perceived by the Spaniards. The Spaniards were not, after all, anthropologists. Nor did the concept of culture as we now know it exist in anyone's mind.

With the advantage of hindsight and through careful use of information that has come to us from documentary history, anthropological studies among living O'odham, ethnology, oral history, archaeology, and the principles of ecology it becomes possible at least to imagine what some of the ethnographic realities of O'odham culture may have been in the late seventeenth century when it began to be heavily impacted by European-derived influences.

First of all, there appear to have been a trio of major—and quite different—modes of adaptation to the Sonoran Desert by its O'odham inhabitants. These were distinguished by distinctive settlement and activity patterns based on contrasts in availability of food.

The adaptations were necessitated chiefly by three separate rainfall regimes in the region: from zero to five inches in the extremely arid western section where the vegetation is dominated by such small-leaved plants as the creosote bush and bursage; from five to ten inches in a central section—the Sells unit of today's Papago Indian Reservation—whose vegetation is primarily stem succulents such as the saguaro and paloverde; and from ten to fifteen inches in the higher eastern and southern elevations where the San Pedro, Santa Cruz, Babasac, San Miguel, Magdalena, Altar, and other perennial streams afford the greatest abundance and widest variety of plants and animals.

The western third of the Pimería Alta is bounded on the north by the Gila River, on the south by the head of the Gulf of California, on the west by the Tinajas Altas and Gila Mountains paralleling the lower Colorado River, and on the east by the western boundary of today's Papago Indian Reservation. The hottest and driest part of the Pimería, it is where edible plants and animals are in shortest supply. Except for lands adjacent to the only perennial stream (and it is interrupted), the Río Sonoyta, the desert here is inhospitable to horticulture or agriculture. It takes water to make crops grow.

Given the environment, the western O'odham—the so-called Areneños, Sand Papagos, or Hia Ced O'odham—were of necessity almost entirely food collectors rather than food producers. Following the seasons, they had to travel by foot over great expanses of land to glean their basic subsistence: water, wild plants, and native animals. Their existence seems largely to have been a nomadic one. Other than at Sonoyta, where they may have lived and intermarried with other O'odham, their settlements were essentially camping sites. These were the No Village people who, through mobility and by keeping their population small, probably never

numbered more then three or four hundred, were able to take advantage of the comparatively few available resources.

Ethnobiologists have listed some sixty wild plants used by Sand Papagos as food or beverage sources, including saguaro, senita, organ pipe, hedgehog, barrel, prickly pear, and cholla cacti; agave; paloverde, mesquite, ironwood, screwbean, and catclaw; wolfberry; chia; horse purslane; goosefoot; chiltepine; desert spinach; *condalia*; and others. They raised corn, squash, and tepary beans in scattered locations on those rare occasions when direct rainfall permitted, and in historic times they grew wheat, watermelons, grapes, and pomegranates.

Edible insects included locusts, cicadas, sphinx moth larvae, and army worms, while ocean spiders, sea turtles, shrimps, clams, sea bass, and other fish could be gotten from the shoreline on the Gulf of California. Lizards, iguanas, chuckwallas, desert tortoises, antelope, ringtails, jackrabbits, wood rats, deer, squirrels, badgers, bobcats, kit foxes, bighorn sheep, and gophers were potential food sources as were ducks, herons, quails, coots, and doves.

The only place in this western region where Spaniards built a mission church, San Marcelo, was at Sonoyta on the Río Sonoyta, a

O'odham family south of Santa Ana, Sonora, 1894. Wm. Dinwiddie

An O'odham woman grinding corn at San Xavier del Bac, 1894. Wm. Dinwiddie

place of reliable water where the largest number of O'odham were congregated. It was a short-lived venture. The Jesuit missionary, Enrique Ruhen, was installed here in 1751 when the place was re-named San Miguel. He was killed that November in a general uprising of Northern Pimans and the mission was never re-established. The Jesuit church is today but a crumbled ruin, a mound of melted earth alongside a dusty road. The adjoining O'odham settlement, too, is gone.

The riverless heart of the Pimería Alta, the aboriginal domain of the Papago Indians, or Tohono O'odham, was referred to by Spaniards as the Papaguería.

The O'odham who lived here may have been subdivided into as many as a half dozen dialect groups, each comprised of people related by blood or by marriage.

This region of today's main body of the Papago Indian Reservation normally receives from five to ten inches of rainfall annually, at least half coming June through August. This is enough water to make summer flash-flood farming (*ak chin* or *de temporal* agriculture) of the intermontane valleys a practical pursuit. During the torrential summer downpours, every mountainside and foothills arroyo becomes a water delivery ditch carrying the sudden moisture and organic nutrients onto the plains between the mountain ranges. By building brush weirs at the mouths of these arroyos, people were able to lift the water onto the surrounding fields to water seeds planted by digging stick. But because the valleys are devoid of surface water except after rains, the O'odham were forced to live much of the year in winter villages located next to springs or shallow wells in the foothills of desert mountain ranges. During the summer rainy season, when farming could take place, they moved to a summer field (*oidak*) to plant, tend, and harvest corn, squash, and beans. Such horticulture, the products of which may have supplied about 20 percent of the food supply, was supplemented by the seasonal gathering of wild plant products and hunting for game. Subsistence was further augmented through trade, with people walking to visit other Indians who might be better supplied with crops but who needed salt, labor, ceremonial performances, or animal hides.

This pattern of moving from a winter "well" village to a summer "field" village resulted in a Two Village people. Spaniards who encountered these O'odham regarded them as being nomadic and seldom understood why villages were sometimes fully occupied but abandoned at other times. Such migratory tendencies on the part of these O'odham also discouraged missionaries from trying to build permanently manned mission stations among them. Although most Papaguerian villages were given saints' names, none ever had a resident priest in the periods during which Spain and Mexico ruled the land.

The largest and most firmly anchored northern O'odham communities were those near perennial streams along the perimeters of the Pimería Alta: the San Pedro, Cocóspera, upper San Miguel, Santa Cruz, Magdalena, Altar, and Concepción. Farming here could generally be assured

during the summer simply by planting crops at the edges of the rivers' floodplains and communities could grow as much as 40 percent of their needed food. It is uncertain whether ditches were dug in pre-Spanish times to carry water to fields.

Water is the powerful magnet in deserts, and rivers attracted the largest and most varied plant and animal communities. Hunting and gathering were therefore easier. And because water was available year around, seasonal migrations were unnecessary.

When Father Kino and other missionaries arrived in the Pimería Alta, they found the largest settlements next to the rivers. These were settlements with such names as Átil, Buquivaba, Bísanig, Búsani, Caborca, Cabórica, Cocóspera, Guevavi, Ímuris, Oquitoa, Pitiquín (Pitiquito), Sáric, Tucson, Tubutama, and Tumacácori. In bringing these communities under the Christian umbrella, missionaries assigned them saints' names as well: San Francisco de Asís, María Magdalena, San Valentín, San Ambrosio, Nuestra Señora de la Purísima Concepción, San Ignacio, Nuestra Señora del Pilar y Santiago, Los Santos Ángeles, San José, San Antonio, San Diego, Santa Gertrudis, San Cosme, San Pedro y San Pablo, and San Cayetano.

It was among the One Village

people that the Jesuit and Franciscan missionaries lived and constructed their churches. The largest of these settlements in the late seventeenth century was Wa:k, or Bac, where in 1692 Father Kino bestowed the patronage of San Francisco Xavier, the Jesuit Apostle to the Indies.

O'odham Culture in the Pimería Alta.

When Spain's missionaries arrived on the northern frontier of New Spain in the Sonoran Desert, it seems never to have occurred to the early arrivals that the native peoples among whom they labored possessed what today

An O'odham woman with a burden basket at San Xavier del Bac, 1894. Wm. Dinwiddie

Four stages in building an O'odham menstrual seclusion hut at San Xavier del Bac, 1894.
Wm. Dinwiddie

would be called a "culture." The attitude on the part of missionaries was instead that the native peoples were as blank slates waiting to have written on them, not only the word of God, but the words of Western civilization as these were understood by its representatives in the late seventeenth and early eighteenth centuries. Moreover, for these words the natives, who were terribly deprived in the minds of Europeans, should be everlastingly grateful. In the twentieth century we call this attitude one of ethnocentrism, an idea that existed in no one's head—European or Native American—in previous centuries.

The evidence suggests that except in the instance of native curing practices and aboriginal polygamy, missionaries and other Europeans never believed they were replacing native culture with something else. Their efforts, they believed, were not a matter of substitution. They were instead a matter of teaching, of giving a people those things concerning which they had no previous knowledge: the good news of Jesus Christ and knowledge, for example, of the "correct" modes of dress, of building shelters, of laying out towns, of political governance, of farming methods, of curing, of accounting and economy, of time keeping, of daily routine, and of social relationships. Even the natives' language, incapable of expressing such ideas as the Holy Trinity and mysteries of the rosary, was thought by many early missionaries to be deficient.

Lessons were to be taught by instruction, example, and, if necessary, by coercion—but always for the spiritual and temporal best interest of the Indians. The missionary effort, enlightened by its own standards, was nothing if not sincere.

It now seems clear, however, that the O'odham had spent hundreds of years evolving successful adaptations to their Sonoran Desert environs and that until they were set upon by European intruders, these adaptations afforded a way of life satisfactory to them.

Their villages, whether in the Papaguería or along the rivers, appeared to Spaniards as random, disorganized scatterations of brush huts. There were no plazas, no streets, no contiguous dwellings, and no buildings of any permanence. What existed instead were private family structures arranged in family compounds. These consisted of brush houses and storage units, a cooking enclosure, and a sunshade (ramada or *vato*) consisting of a flat roof supported on four or more posts. They were sited to afford privacy from neighbors and with consideration of drainage.

The only public structure in a village was a round brush building called the rain house (*vahki*), round house (*olas ki*), or big house (*gu ki*). It was here men held their nightly council meetings where matters were decided by consensus. It was also here that ceremonial paraphernalia were stored and where preparations were made for such ceremonies as the all-important annual saguaro wine feast, essential for bringing rain. The public ceremonies themselves were held on cleared grounds opposite the east-facing entrance of the rain house.

The rain house was centrally located in the village because the town crier would climb in the morning either onto its roof or onto the roof of its adjoining ramada to shout out instructions for the day's activities: a rabbit hunt, clearing fields, gathering wood, or whatever the community chores might be. Family dwellings had to be within earshot of the rain house.

O'odham architecture, moreover, was dry—a practical consideration in an arid land. Mesquite, grass, ribs of saguaro cacti, and similar plant materials were used in building structures. If one wanted a mud roof, one simply put dirt on the top and waited for rain. And structures were practical

Tohono O'odham Danny Lopez stands by a rain house in the O'odham village of Gu Oidak (Big Fields), 1980. Bernard Fontana

Tohono O'odham Clara Lopez weaves a basket at her home. Bernard Fontana

in another way. To build them was not labor intensive and to give them up, either permanently or temporarily, caused no great sacrifice to individual or community. O'odham, who slept and cooked out of doors except in inclement weather, rested lightly upon their landscape.

Village headmen held office by dint of their abilities rather than through inheritance. These abilities were expressed in various titles for the office: Wise Speaker (ritual orator), Keeper of the Smoke (organizer and principal speaker at council meetings), Keeper of the Plaited Basket (the person in charge of the group's sacred bundle), and The One Above (a person with "great man" status). Community decisions were made via consensus of adult males. The headman was more moderator and conciliator than authoritarian figure. He assuredly could not function as an autocrat.

There were men who assisted the headman in various tasks and there were others who were in charge on special occasions: war leader, song leader, hunt leader, and game leader, for example. Moreover, each village with its small group of descended villages was autonomous. Except in times of war or the threat of war, there was no over-arching leadership among the O'odham.

O'odham economy was based on the notion of generosity and sharing. Ceremonial exchanges, gifts, and betting on inter-village games were means of distributing available resources as evenly as possible throughout the entire polity. Stinginess was one of the worst vices one could have. Although O'odham subsisted in an environment of scarcity, they behaved as if they lived surrounded by abundance. People invested in relatives, friends, and neighbors rather than in material wealth. Cooperation was the key to desert survival. Men and women, moreover, shared much of the work. Family and community were one's insurance.

All Piman life came together in a concept known as *o'odham hímdag*, the Piman Way. It would be a mistake to translate *o'odham hímdag* as Piman Indian religion because *hímdag* (way) encompasses the whole way of life. O'odham had no religion separate and apart from their daily activities. Their animistic belief was that various mammals, insects, amphibians, birds, and reptiles, as well as lightning, wind, ocean, enemies, and "women of the darkness" (harlots) also had *hímdag* as well as potentially dangerous *géwkadag* (strength). This ideology did much to moderate daily behavior even as it

afforded a workable explanation for a whole class of illnesses. The essence of *hímdag* was in nearly all things, all people, and all actions—public and private (curing) ceremonies included.

Important public ceremonies were connected with crops, hunting, warfare, community well being, and, most important of all, "bringing down the clouds." It was rain that meant life in the desert, and a great deal of religious energy was directed toward invoking that blessing.

Although many Spanish missionaries regarded the O'odham language as lacking in its ability to express the precepts of Christian belief and doctrine, language was perhaps the O'odham's highest form of art. Speeches, ritual oratory, and song lyrics were powerful and poetic. Moreover, the grammar of the language is as subtle and complex as any in the world; its vocabulary is rich in words defining the external and internal world of the O'odham.

"In short," as Daniel Matson and the present author have written elsewhere, "the Piman Indians whom the missionaries encountered in the late seventeenth century in (what became) northern Sonora had political organizations, social organizations, economic organizations, a complex language, and a religion which was the embodiment of their various ways of life. They had developed a technology admirably adapted to desert subsistence, one which appears to have been well suited to extracting a maximal living from the natural surroundings while imposing the least amount of long-ranged environmental damage."[1]

Their existence, however, was far from Utopian. Food supplies were often precarious and there were surely times of starvation. Life expectancy was probably short. And it is also some measure of the quality of their existence when one takes into account their ready acceptance of many plants, animals, and artifacts—if not ideas—brought by those who would make Spaniards of them. But that is another story.

Where Are the O'odham Now?

What has become of the Indians who once lived in the communities of the Pimería Alta and in whose villages Jesuit and Franciscan missionaries built houses of Christian worship? The only such Pimería Alta settlement today whose population, about 1,300, remains almost totally O'odham is that of Wa:k (Bac). Franciscans now administer the Mission of San Xavier del Bac for descendants of the people for whom Father Kino founded the mission in 1692. Other O'odham live in Tucson and in villages scattered throughout the vast 2,700,000-acre reservation in Arizona that is home for the Tohono O'odham Nation, and which combines three non-contiguous units: San Xavier (created in 1874), Gila Bend (1882), and Sells (1916). The nation's headquarters is in Sells.

The River People, the so-called Pimas of Arizona and among whom Spanish missionaries never gained a foothold, occupy parts of the Gila River (1859) and Salt River (1879) reservations south and east of Phoenix, while a mixed population of Tohono O'odham (Papagos) and Pimas live on the Ak Chin (or Maricopa) Reservation (1912) west of Maricopa, Arizona. In total, there are possibly more than twenty-five thousand O'odham who continue to live in the United States, both on and off reservations.

The story in Sonora is quite different. Except in Caborca, where a few O'odham remain, former settlements where missions have not been abandoned—places like Santa Cruz, Ímuris, San Ignacio, Magdalena, Tubutama, Átil, Oquitoa, and Pitiquito—are homes for *Mexicanos* rather than for *Indios*. It has been this way since at least the middle of the nineteenth century. By 1801, it was asserted there were no O'odham any longer resident in Ímuris. The non-Indian population of the San Ignacio district rose from 306 in 1801 to 1,471 by 1820. O'odham at Caborca protested in 1835 that Caborca, Saric, Tubutama, and Oquitoa were being taken over by Mexican settlers. By the late 1840s, most O'odham south of today's international boundary had either assimilated into Mexican culture, becoming *Mexicanos* in the process, or had abandoned the river towns for areas farther out in the desert or to seek work on ranches and in mines. In 1842 and again in 1898, O'odham suffered military defeats at the hands of Mexicans, and after 1898 most Sonoran O'odham chose to migrate to the United States. A census conducted by Mexico's National Indian Institute in 1979 enumerated 197 Papagos still living permanently in Sonora. Today many of these people reside at Quitovac on lands reserved for their use and occupancy.

The cultural assimilation of O'odham in Sonora came about through peaceful, if unfair, means rather than militarily. The dismemberment of mission properties that occurred in the Pimería Alta after 1828 led to the privatization of lands, undermined the native tradition of communal subsistence, and led to an increased demand for Indian labor in a cash economy. This foreordained that Indians would mix more readily with Spanish, mestizo, and mulatto settlers who by then comprised the majority population. The movement toward Mexicanization, with entry at the bottom rung of the socioeconomic ladder, became an inevitability.

Bernard L. Fontana

NEW SPAIN'S NORTHWESTERN FRONTIER

BY
MARDITH SCHUETZ–MILLER

From the very beginning of civilization in Europe the elite looked to exotic countries for luxury goods: gold, ivory, and slaves from Africa, silks from China, gems and spices from Southeast Asia. Since historic times these goods had been controlled by Semitic traders, while Italian maritime city–states such as Venice and Genoa grew rich as intermediaries in the trade. During the early Renaissance, Portugal emerged as Europe's first great naval power. Portugal's inexorable advance toward the sources of desired luxury items began with her colonizing the Azores and Madeiras in the 1430s and then establishing slaving stations down the west coast of Africa. In 1488 Bartolomé Díaz rounded the Cape of Good Hope and a decade later Vasco de Gama not only repeated the feat, but reached India. Portugal was finally

Facing page: engraving from Bernardo de Vargas Machuca, Milicia y Descripción de las Indias. Madrid, 1599

in a position to cut out both the Italian merchants and the hated Muslim middlemen. Access to the Spice Islands via the Indian Ocean having been preempted by the Portuguese, Columbus proposed to the Spanish monarchs Ferdinand and Isabela that Spain might share in the prize by sailing in the opposite direction—that is, sailing westward to reach China.

Exploration and Colonization.

The final acceptance by the Spanish king and queen of Columbus's astounding proposal and his discovery of the New World in 1492 is familiar enough, but the goal of cashing in on the wealth of the Orient, which long persisted, is forgotten in the exciting history of the conquest of these new lands that followed. Columbus may have gone to his grave holding to his belief that he had indeed reached the Orient, but his sixteenth century successors knew better and continued the search.

Within the first quarter of the sixteenth century the enormousness of the American continent became known to the Spaniards. Vasco Núñez de Balboa ventured across the Isthmus of Panama in 1513 and viewed the Pacific Ocean. Ferdinand Magellan actually sailed through the straits off the tip of South America which bear his name and entered the waters of the Pacific in 1520. Within another five years, Spanish navigators had explored the Atlantic coast of North America from Labrador to Florida and the coast of the Caribbean from Florida to Panama. Although it had not been located, everyone remained convinced of the existence of the Straits of Anian or the Northwest Passage that would cut directly across the continent and link Atlantic to Pacific. Its importance to the crown was voiced by Hernán Cortez, México's conqueror, in a letter to his king:

. . . if it should please God that the said strait be found . . . the voyage from the spice region to your kingdom would be very easy and very short, so much so that it would be less than two-thirds that the route now followed, and that without any risks to the vessels coming and going, because they would always come and go through your dominions, so that in case of necessity they could be repaired without danger whenever they might wish to enter port.

Cortez's efforts to discover the straits were concentrated on the Pacific. Between 1527 and 1539 he instigated five maritime explorations of the Pacific coast, including his personal failed attempt to colonize Baja California in 1535.

Important to Sonora history was the Cortez-sponsored voyage undertaken in 1539 by Francisco de Ulloa, who sailed to the head of *El Mar Vermejo* (the Vermilion Sea), which we know today either as the Sea of Cortez or the Gulf of California. From the head of the gulf, he coasted Baja California and proved it to be a peninsula. Curiously, this early knowledge of the peninsula was suppressed, and the long arm of Baja California came to be depicted as an island on early maps of North America. This remained the case until Father Eusebio Francisco Kino once again proved its true nature at the beginning of the eighteenth century.

The greatest incentive to sixteenth century colonization of California should have been the development of the long-sought oriental trade that Spain finally realized with its subjugation of the Philippines in 1571, fifty years after Magellan had claimed the islands for the crown. Ports were needed to repair and reprovision the galleons engaged in this Manila trade and to restore the health of seamen scurvy-bedeviled from the long voyage which, on the return, might take up to six months. Furthermore, a port and coastal patrol were needed to protect the fleet from English and Dutch piracy. In spite of the fact that the 1542–1543 maritime expedition of Juan Rodríguez Cabrillo and Bartolomé Ferrer had explored as far north as Oregon's Rogue River and discovered San Diego Bay, which would have been ideal for the needed port, King Philip II failed to follow through. In a story to be repeated throughout its three-hundred-year control over New Spain, the special needs of the crown's foreign territories would be secondary to more pressing issues at home.

It was under Philip II that the Spanish Empire attained its greatest size. The union of Ferdinand and Isabela in the fifteenth century began the process of unifying the disparate kingdoms of Spain. When their grandson Carlos I was named Holy Roman Emperor in 1519, just two years after ascending the Spanish throne, Spain suddenly had suzerainty over Flanders, the German–Hungarian states, much of France and Italy, and North Africa in addition to her territories in the New World, the Marianas, and the Philippines. And when Carlos I's son, Philip II, also inherited the Portuguese Empire in 1581, a quarter century after succeeding his father as king, Spain then controlled West Africa, Brazil, and Portuguese claims in Southeast Asia and the Pacific. Trying to hold together this unwieldy empire drained the immense wealth of silver that had flowed from the New World to the old.

When Philip II's weak son Philip III succeeded his father in 1598, the empire began to crumble. A French–Dutch alliance threatened Flanders. Italian city–states divided and switched their loyalties between Spain and France, while the Austrian branch plunged into the Thirty Years War.

Proselytizing, Prospecting, and Conflict.

Spanish America had problems of its own with its readily accessible silver veins playing out and a severe labor shortage hampering progress and a movement toward less dependence on the mother country. Yet another reason why Spain failed to follow through on colonizing California was the abatement of English piracy following the death of Elizabeth I in 1603. For the time being, European powers had problems closer to home and development of the Pacific could wait.

In the meantime, early reports of rich kingdoms to the north lured Spanish explorers from Mexico City to New Mexico in 1539 and 1540. Simultaneously, a succession of silver strikes drew miners, adventurers, and settlers to Zacatecas, Durango, Hidalgo, Guanajuato, Aguascalientes, San Luis Potosí, and Chihuahua for the next twenty years. *Presidios* (military posts) and fortified towns evolved to protect the mines and silver-laden caravans carrying bullion to Mexico City. Missions were established by both Franciscans and Jesuits to effect the conversion of the Indians. The arrival of slave traders and riffraff, attracted by the new wealth, ruled out the possibility of peaceful coexistence between Spaniards and indigenous populations. Nevertheless, by the end of the century the occupation of New Mexico had been undertaken and the silver quest had led Spaniards to within a stone's throw of other areas of the present United States–Mexico border.

As the sixteenth century was drawing to a close the Jesuits looked to the Pacific coast for new mission territory. Beginning in 1591 from Culiacán, Sinaloa, they enjoyed a century of advance northward, working and proselytizing among the native settlements concentrated along the river valleys of the Fuerte, Mayo, and Yaqui. As early as the 1620s they were reaching the Lower Pima, Opata, and Jova, but a seventy-five-year hiatus was to ensue before Father Kino would begin his labors among the Upper Pima. Between 1683 and 1686 another attempt was made to establish a permanent Spanish outpost in Baja California, a failed venture in which the crown promptly lost interest but which fired the zeal of one of its participants, Father Kino. The Jesuits, having persuaded the crown to allow them to undertake colonization of the peninsula at their own expense, successfully established the first settlement at Loreto in 1697. While the Jesuits readied for their project on the west side of the Gulf, Kino was ordered north to begin work among the Upper Pima in 1687.

Peace in the northwest territory was doomed as Spaniards began slowly to reach into Sonora in the 1640s, a pace which quickened when prospectors, gripped by silver fever, augmented mining

Spanish coin, 1598, bearing the shield of King Philip II (1556–1598).

Spanish galleons.

operations in 1660. The predictable conflicts arose as growing Spanish and mestizo populations usurped the more favorable land and forced indigenous peoples into less desirable areas.

Conflicts in other regions of New Spain's northern borderlands had repercussions in Sonora. Most of the Pueblo Indians of New Mexico rebelled against Spanish oppression and actually ousted the settlers from the province in 1680. Their success inflamed other Indians to follow suit. Jocomes, Sumas, Janos, and Apaches threatened Spanish towns, ranches, and mines across northern Chihuahua and Sonora, and the *presidio* of Santa Rosa de Corodéhuachi (Fronteras) was established in 1690 in an effort to contain them. The first *Compañía Volante* was stationed there three years later. This Flying Company of cavalry was an innovative approach designed for immediate response to the mounted and rapidly moving native warriors of the border.

However, larger conflicts among competing European nations also affected New Spain's northern frontier. By the end of the seventeenth century, three colonial powers were vying for territorial expansion. England had established colonies along the Atlantic seaboard from New York to the Carolinas, the latter a threat to Spanish Florida. France had control of Canada and was busy consolidating claims to the Mississippi Valley, hammering an effective wedge between New Spain's eastern and western claims to the entire Gulf Coast. Robert Cavelier, Sieur de La Salle, established an outpost on the Texas coast in 1685. That act resulted in a half-hearted attempt by Spaniards to occupy Texas beginning in 1690. But it was only after France had founded New Orleans and successfully attacked Spanish Pensacola in a new outbreak of hostilities in 1719 that the Spanish crown committed itself wholeheartedly to stopping the French at the western Louisiana border.

Why had there been such a delay in Spain's efforts to colonize Texas? A major reason was that her attention had been diverted toward protecting Florida after the English invaded its Apalachee country in 1703.

In addition to the attacks on her northeastern borderlands, Spain became threatened on her unprotected northwestern flank when rumors reached the Spanish court that Russians were planting settlements down the Pacific coast. Simultaneously, the English had wrested control of Canada from France and were said to be pushing westward across their new territory to plant warehouses on the coast to expand the lucrative fur trade. Once again, the decision to colonize a long-held Spanish claim, upper California in this instance, was dictated by international politics and economic conditions. The Spanish occupation of Alta California was finally undertaken in 1769.

By the middle of the eighteenth century it had become obvious that the continuing problems, both internal and external, that beset Spain's northern borderlands called for a new approach if the challenge were to be met successfully. King Carlos III dispatched his Visitor General José de Gálvez to inspect the frontier and recommend changes. As a result, the area from California to Texas was mapped in 1771. *Presidios* were realigned the following year in the mistaken belief that a cordon of posts set more or less at equal intervals would form an impenetrable barrier against attacks by hostile Indians north of that line. Most important was the creation in 1776 of a *comandancia general*, a general command for the Interior Provinces (*Provincias Internas*) which could deal directly with the Council of the Indies in Spain rather than routing action communications through the viceroy in Mexico City. It was presumed this separate military government

El Caballero de Croix, first commander of the Provincias Internas. From Alfred B. Thomas, Teodoro de Croix

would be in a position to respond more quickly to the unique problems of the northern provinces. Don Teodoro de Croix, the first Commandant General, established his capital in Arizpe, Sonora, in late 1779.

The hope for a peaceful frontier quickly faded. The new military government might have succeeded had Spain provided sufficient personnel and financial resources to implement orders. The New Regulations of 1772 for *presidios*, for example, called for a war of extermination against the Apaches who were threatening the border from Texas to Sonora. However, adequate resources of men and materiel were not forthcoming. The royal treasury was drained partially because of Spain's commitment to the American Revolution against England. As a result, a royal order issued fourteen years later called instead for a program of pacification that would be less costly to the crown. The northern borderlands had always been little more than a pawn on the international chessboard and would continue in this situation until Mexico gained her independence from Spain in 1821. Spanish presence in the Pimería Alta, as in other border regions, owed its beginnings to affairs in the rest of the world. This international linkage, one that deeply affected the native population, remained until the end.

JESUITS AND FRANCISCANS

BY
KIERAN R. McCARTY, O.F.M.

It was a Papal Bull of Julian II promulgated in 1508 that laid the groundwork for Jesuit and Franciscan missionary endeavors in the Pimería Alta. It established the principle of *patronato real*, or royal patronage, a legally regulated grant by the church to the Spanish crown. The crown became the pope's representative in the Spanish New World primarily because of its willingness to support the missionary endeavor with funds from the royal treasury. Thus it was that missionaries, whose principal task was to bring word of the good news of Christ to the uninitiated, also became agents of the Spanish king. They were appointed to bring about the cultural assimilation of the native population. The end result of this process was expected to be a God-fearing and tax-paying subject of Spain. So was the Indian thus enlightened expected to pay

ecclesiastical tithes to support the parish priest and local bishop.

As long as Native Americans were under the aegis of missionaries, all of whom were so-called regular clergy, members of religious orders, they were exempt from both civil taxes and ecclesiastical tithes. It was only after they became fully formed Christians and subjects of the crown that they joined the ranks of all other tax-paying subjects in having their religious affairs administered by secular clergy, priests who lived in the world and who stood in the ordinary hierarchy of the church.

In the Pimería Alta, first Jesuits and, after them, Franciscans found themselves pressured by both secular religious authorities and by civil and military authorities to hasten the process of christianization. The fact remains, however, that from beginning to end of Spain's hegemony in the region, the O'odham of the Pimería Alta remained a responsibility of regular, rather than secular, clergy and the desired assimilation failed to take place.

The Society of Jesus.

It was the end of the seventeenth century when the so-called Jesuit period of the Pimería Alta began. Eusebio Francisco Kino, a Jesuit missionary from the Italian Tyrol, was the first resident priest in what he himself labelled the Pimería Alta. Arriving in 1687 at the southernmost Upper Piman village of Cosari or Bamotze, which he appended with the Christian name of *Nuestra Señora de los Dolores* (Our Lady of Sorrows) after a painting he had brought with him, the black-robed pioneer Jesuit worked from this base for twenty-four years. He founded missions and mission districts as far north as what is now Tucson, Arizona, until his death in March of 1711 at Magdalena, Sonora, where he is buried.

The ideals and the spirit of Kino and his fellow Jesuits were the product of the baroque sixteenth century, the Age of Power, the Age of Pragmatism. Their approach to Indian missions, as well as to any other task they undertook, was eminently practical. They maintained large haciendas and ranchos in central Mexico to support materially the frontier missions, such as those in the Pimería Alta. Kino himself mirrored and aided the central Mexico effort by founding sizeable

The birthplace of Father Eusebio Francisco Kino in Segno, Italy, 1990. Mardith Schuetz-Miller

cattle ranches of his own on the frontier. Thus he has become famous as the cowboy missionary, a horseman par excellence.

As early as 1591, the Society of Jesus (Jesuits) began its missions along Mexico's northwest coast near the mouth of the Sinaloa River, culminating nearly a hundred years later in Kino's Pimería Alta many leagues to the north. In all, Kino founded eight mission districts (*partidos*), with satellite mission stations in each. These stretched from his mission headquarters of Dolores on the San Miguel River in the south to the Gila River (near present-day Phoenix) on the north, and from the San Pedro River on the east to the Colorado River on the west.

His method was to encourage the traditional settled villages in their age-old practice of seasonal planting up and down the rivers. The pattern observed by the people themselves from ancient times was to establish what we might call a permanent village on a piece of higher ground, safe from flooding. Then, as the rains annually washed out a field or two from previous years, they would choose another section of the river to do their planting and set up a temporary field village to tend to the new crop. Inexperienced travelers were sometimes confused by these temporary field villages, and in their reports and diaries would confuse later chroniclers into recording them as permanent settlements. Kino established missions proper only at permanent village sites, as can be seen by the positioning of the famous churches throughout the Pimería Alta. Only Caborca seems to have been placed too low along the river.

It is significant to note that Kino added considerably to native nourishing crops by introducing winter wheat, which not only gave the native diet extra nourishment, but added winter as a new time for planting. Native crops of corn, beans, and squash could be

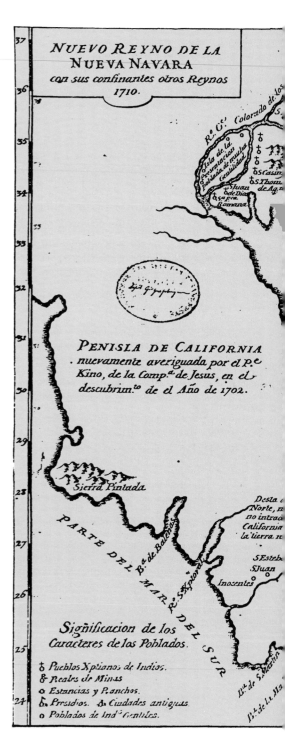

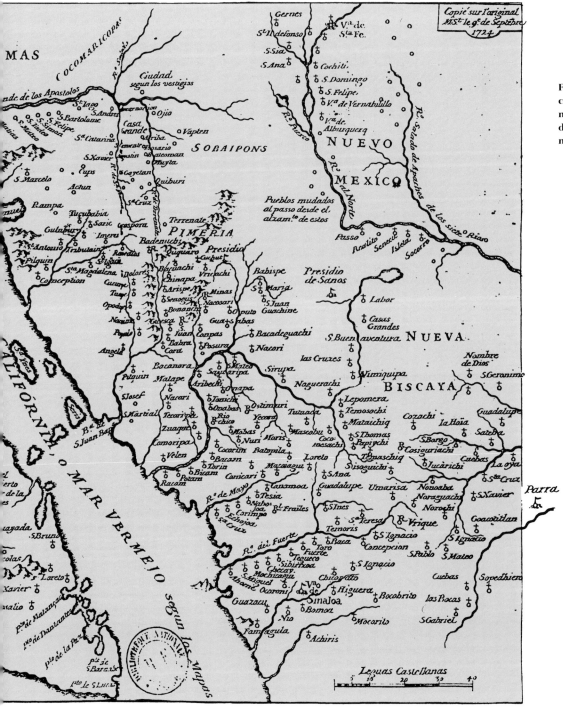

Father Kino, a cartographer of considerable talent, drew this map in 1710 shortly before his death. (Shown here is a copy made in 1724.)

Brass crucifix, 1¾″ high, excavated from Mission Guevavi. Dick P. Hsu

Ruins of Mission Guevavi, 1889. George Roskruge

grown only in the summer. The proof of the popularity of Kino's innovation lies in the predominance in the Pimería Alta of the wheat-flour tortilla over the traditional central-Mexican corn tortilla.

Spanish cattle were perhaps Kino's most spectacular addition to the native food supply, and it is said to this day it is the industry the natives of the Pimería Alta accomplish best. It is one that can even be called a family industry.

It was in this exciting new complex of village life that Kino and his fellow Jesuits introduced the building of Christian churches and the catechetical instruction that accompanied them. Since what some choose to call "native religion" was, and is, mainly native beliefs and ceremonies related to "bringing down the clouds" and to the curing or avoidance of physical ills, the spiritual realm of Christian saints and divinity had little difficulty taking its place in the native way, *o'odham hímdag*, and today bears a name equally traditional: *sá:nto hímdag* or saints' way.

Despite the success and attractiveness of the Kino years between 1687 and 1711 in the Pimería Alta, at no time during those twenty-four years were more than three or four Jesuits sent to help him cover this vast territory. Even these came at intervals, and some did not stay.

There was one notable exception. Father Agustín de Campos, Kino's closest confrere, manned the San Ignacio mission for more than thirty years. Within his jurisdiction was the Magdalena *visita* (visiting station) where Kino went on March 15, 1711, to dedicate a devotional chapel to his own favorite saint, San Francisco Xavier. While there, he became ill and died shortly after midnight "with great peace," as Father Campos wrote. Father Kino's remains, under glass and a domed enclosure, can be seen today in the memorial plaza in Magdalena precisely where Father Campos laid him to rest.

After Kino's death, Pimería Alta Jesuits were barely able to maintain the status quo, and much less to effect the advances planned by Kino. For nearly a decade, Father Campos without helpers ministered to the middle corridor from San Ignacio and Magdalena northward; his sole companion, Father Luis Velarde, attended the eastern area, including Dolores. The west, from Sáric and Tubutama to Caborca, was abandoned.

In 1720, two Sicilian Jesuits came to attend the western sector. In 1731, three northern Europeans arrived to provide a resident missionary for Soamca, Guevavi, and San Xavier del Bac. These were the northernmost missions established by Kino, and they all lay along the same river, one named the Río Santa María by Kino for the mission at its headwaters, Santa María de Soamca. Later, a Spanish military post named Santa Cruz was situated in that same region and the name of the river was changed to that by which it is known today.

With other Jesuits who arrived soon after, the eight traditional mission districts initially founded by Kino now had resident missionaries. Stockraising and building proceeded apace.

A major native uprising in 1751 temporarily halted the

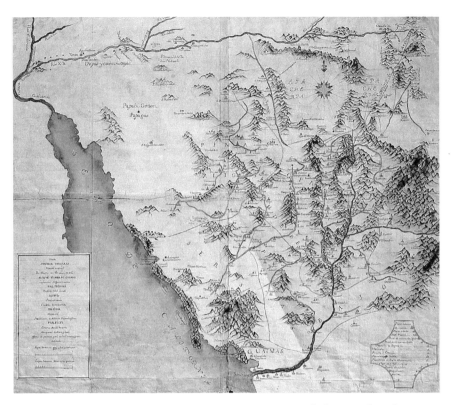

Hanc Sonora Tabulum, attributed to Juan Nentvig, ca. 1792. Courtesy Museo Naval, Madrid, Spain

action. Led by an Indian from Sáric named Luis Oacpicagigua, many Northern O'odham rose against their Spanish overseers and Jesuit missionaries, killing Father Tomás Tello at Caborca and Father Enrique Ruhen at Sonoyta in the process. They also killed at least an additional hundred Spaniards and Indians friendly to the Spanish cause. But the rebellion was quelled early in 1752 by Spanish soldiers and progress in building, expansion, and exploration continued.

It was only the European politics of 1767 that thwarted what would have been a glorious future for the Jesuit missions of the Pimería Alta. By an order issued by King Carlos III of Spain in June 1767 the Society of Jesus was exiled from all Spanish lands. The reasons were complex, but none of them were justified and absolutely none of them lessened the lustre of Kino and the Jesuits of the Pimería Alta.

Finding Father Kino

On February 14, 1965, on the fifty-third anniversary of Arizona's admission to the union as a state, a larger-than-life-size bronze statue of Father Eusebio Francisco Kino was dedicated and presented as the last of Arizona's two representatives in the Rotunda of the United States Capitol. (The other is a statue of copper magnate John C. Greenway). Among the distinguished guests at the unveiling and dedication ceremony was the Honorable Hugo Margín, ambassador from Mexico. It was possibly the ambassador who alerted Mexican President Gustavo Díaz Ordaz that Americans were paying singular homage to a man who belonged as much to Sonora and Mexico as he did to Arizona and the United States.

Soon after, President Díaz Ordaz charged his Secretary of Public Education, Agustín Yáñez, with the task of locating and positively identifying Father Kino's mortal remains, a job which the secretary assigned on June 30 to Professor Wigberto Jiménez Moreno, head of the Department of Historical Research of Mexico's National Institute of Anthropology and History.

Beginning in August 1965, a half year after the statue's dedication, an international team of investigators headed by Jiménez Moreno arrived in Magdalena, where it was known Father Kino had died in 1711, to begin the search on the ground. It was a hunt that had gone on sporadically at least since 1922 when Bishop Juan Navarette tried without success to locate the grave site.

In addition to Jiménez Moreno, the principal investigators were Jorge Olvera H., an art and architecture historian with a background in archaeology; Arturo Romano P., physical anthropologist; Jorge Angula, archaeologist; Sonoran historians Fernando Pesqueira and Father Cruz Acuña; cartographer Conrado Gallegos; chemist Gabriel Sánchez de la Vega; and Americans William W. Wasley, archaeologist, and Father Kieran R. McCarty, O.F.M., historian.

As work proceeded, it became known from documentary and published sources that Father Kino had died at the age of sixty-five on the night of March 15, 1711, and had been buried on the Gospel side of the altar between the second and third ashlars (foundation stones) in the new chapel he had just dedicated to San Francisco Xavier. It was also learned that the year after Kino's death two other Jesuits were exhumed from their original burial places in Tubutama and their bones, in a jumble, were reburied on the Epistle and Gospel sides of the church. In 1739, Spaniard Salvador de Noriega was buried at the entrance to the chapel, and in 1837, José Gabriel Vega was buried beneath the nave. In 1828, Father José Pérez Llera had put a stone buttress next to part of the slumping east wall of the chapel.

As work in archives and libraries proceeded, so did work in the field. Members of the team looked carefully at the construction materials and techniques used at the ruins of Remedios, a church known to have been built by Father Kino. So did they examine the adobe walls and stone foundations at Cocóspera and carry out excavations in Magdalena in places where earlier excavations had occurred, and where their own sense of the unfolding evidence took them.

Finally, it was Jorge Olvera and his expert reading of three nineteenth-century depictions of Magdalena—those by John Russell Bartlett (1852), John Ross Browne (1864), and Alphonse Pinart (1879)—that enabled the excavators to zero in on the most likely location of Father Kino's chapel. These drawings indicated the location of Father Agustín Campos's 1705 church in relation to the 1832 church of Father Pérez Llera (the one presently in use), and to Father Kino's chapel. The location of the latter proved to be in an area immediately next to the city hall.

On May 19, 1966, Father Kino's bones were found. He lay undisturbed on the Gospel side of the altar between the second and third ashlars precisely as he had been buried some 255 years earlier. Near him were the secondary burials of the two Tubutama Jesuits, and in the nave of the chapel and just beyond its entrance were the primary burials of 1739 and 1837. Father Pérez Llera's buttress was against the outside of the east wall. Examination of the skeleton, moreover, revealed a European male who was at least sixty years old, showed signs of arthritis (Kino had trouble writing and riding in his later years), and who, unmentioned in the documents, had lost two central incisors long before he died (the tooth sockets had grown over). His coffin was gone, but a simple cassock button remained on his breastbone and a small crucifix lay on his collarbone.

The discovery of Father Kino's remains transformed Magdalena. Its name is now officially Magdalena de Kino, and the area where he was found, which once included the city hall and the archaeological remains of Father Campos's early eighteenth-century church, was completely re-designed by architect Francisco Artigus and rebuilt in 1970 and 1971 as the beautiful memorial plaza seen there today.

Bernard L. Fontana

Drawing by Frances O'Brien of Father Kino, 1962.

Plan by Jorge Olvera, drawn by John Messina.

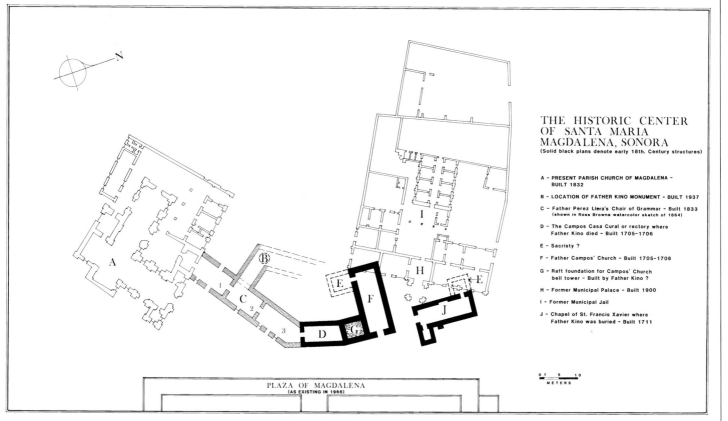

THE HISTORIC CENTER OF SANTA MARIA MAGDALENA, SONORA
(Solid black plans denote early 18th. Century structures)

A – PRESENT PARISH CHURCH OF MAGDALENA – BUILT 1832

B – LOCATION OF FATHER KINO MONUMENT – BUILT 1937

C – Father Perez Llera's Chair of Grammar – Built 1833 (shown in Ross Browne watercolor sketch of 1864)

D – The Campos Casa Cural or rectory where Father Kino died – Built 1705–1706

E – Sacristy ?

F – Father Campos' Church – Built 1705–1706

G – Raft foundation for Campos' Church bell tower – Built by Father Kino ?

H – Former Municipal Palace – Built 1900

I – Former Municipal Jail

J – Chapel of St. Francis Xavier where Father Kino was buried – Built 1711

0 1   5   1 0
METERS

PLAZA OF MAGDALENA
(AS EXISTING IN 1966)

Cross, monogram of Christ, and spikes comprise the Jesuit coat-of-arms.

Franciscan emblem sculptured on the façade of Mission San Xavier del Bac, 1979. Bernard Fontana

The Order of Saint Francis.

The Franciscans, an older Order founded by Saint Francis of Assisi in 1226, had arrived with Columbus on his second voyage and had thereby predated Jesuits in the New World by more than three quarters of a century. They replaced the Jesuits in the Pimería Alta in 1768—with some difficulty since the Franciscan logistical line of missions northward from Mexico City was already stretched to the limit. Nonetheless, they were able to assign a priest to each of the eight principal missions of the Upper Pimería, including an extra man in the case of sickness or death of one of their ranks.

The Society of Jesus in the frontier missions applied the spirit of their times, the seventeenth century Age of Pragmatism, with practical innovations of wheat fields, cattle herds, and thriving commerce. Franciscans, who had arrived in Mexico imbued with the spirit of the sixteenth century Age of Humanism, promoted the Native American art and literature they found in the Valley of Mexico for its human values. Similarly, they left their spiritual message in the Pimería Alta in the form of such visual beauty as seen at Mission San Xavier del Bac with abundant sacred images revealed in its interior decoration.

The leader of the Pimería Alta Franciscan group, Father Antonio Buena y Alcalde, technically known as the Father President (*Padre Presidente*) or praeses, occupied Mission San Pedro y San Pablo de Tubutama. He was also superior of the Lower Pimería missions, but probably chose Tubutama as his residence because it was nearer the frontier and had also been headquarters for the departed Jesuit superior of the Pimería Alta.

For three quarters of a century Franciscans kept the mission frontier of the Pimería Alta alive in the face of formidable change in official government attitude. Jesuit expulsion itself had been proof positive of this change. In keeping with the secularism of the Enlightenment, Carlos III, enlightened despot, and his even more enlightened ministers de-emphasized the role of missionary as Indian agent of the Spanish Crown. Within this same Franciscan period, roughly 1767–1856, the Enlightenment was followed by the Revolutionary and Liberal movements which were even more inimical to religious authority. With increasing openness, the regional bureaucrats of the Pimería Alta often tended to ignore the legitimate requests of the missionaries. It was a difficult period which, however, left its mission glories as well as its mission tragedies.

Certainly the first Franciscan decade's outstanding events, those of 1768–1778 and closely allied to the missions, were the two overland expeditions to the Pacific coast: exploratory in 1774 and in 1776 the colonizing move that resulted in the founding of San Francisco, California.

These expeditions featured two outstanding Franciscan missionaries, the first of whom was Father Pedro Font. Using vestments from mission San Ignacio, he accompanied the colonists all the way to San Francisco and gave that community its name. The long version of his diary of the trek was regarded by the patriarch of western Hispanic historians, Herbert Eugene Bolton, as the best travel diary in the history of the American Southwest. When Father Font returned to Sonora, he first went to the mission at Ures where in June 1776 he completed the short version of his expedition diary and drew the map to accompany it. By November of that year he was stationed in Magdalena when his mission was attacked by Apaches and apostate O'odham. He then went to Tubutama where by May 1777 he completed the diary so highly praised by historian Bolton. Early in 1780, Father Font was stationed at Pitiquito where he completed the graceful church

begun there after 1776 by Father José Matías Moreno. It is a fired brick structure, replete with vaulted and domed ceiling and arches, which remains in use today.

Father Font lies buried in Pitiquito, having died there on September 6, 1781, at the age of forty-three. Comparatively unfamiliar in Sonora and Arizona, he is far better known in California due

to his early descriptions of their land and people.

The other friar, Father Francisco Garcés, is more universally renowned. His basic assignment in the Pimería Alta was at the northernmost mission, San Xavier del Bac, and he was co-founder of the Spanish settlement and *presidio* at Tucson. He left the 1776 colo-

Mission San Xavier del Bac, 1987.
Jack Dykinga

nizing expedition at the Colorado River and explored the interior valleys of California as far north as the Kern River as well as the Hopi country of northern Arizona. He is known as the first European in many areas of Southern California and northwestern Arizona.

Father Garcés returned to San Xavier soon after to help begin the ill-fated Colorado River project at Yuma, the outstanding event of the second decade of Franciscan history in our desert.

There was, and remains, much controversy on whom to lay blame for the Yuma (Quechan) uprising which took place in 1781, the year after Spanish settlements and a mission were established along the Colorado River. One mistake, adduced by many, was that the four Franciscan missionaries led by Father Garcés, who had made contact with the Yumas long before, were deprived—except in purely spiritual matters—of any role in governing the area. This was, of course, in keeping with the secularist domination of the age.

Within three days of the morning of June 17, 1781, when the uprising began, the Yumas had destroyed the Spanish towns, killed many of the soldiers, and beaten the four padres to death with war clubs. The women and children were taken captive, and the commanding officer's wife, Maria Ana Montielo, who was later rescued, recalled in writing "the night my heart was broken, when my beloved husband was clubbed to death before my very eyes." No more missions were attempted along the Colorado River until the coming of modern missionaries in American times.

Beginning in the mid-1770s, the Franciscans embarked upon a spectacular building program which culminated in excellence with the dedication of the church at San Xavier del Bac in 1797. Even the Mexican independence movement that began in 1810 and concluded successfully in 1821 did not deter them from improving their missions to the extent that economic conditions allowed. The building program suffered a severe blow in the late 1820s, however, when Spaniards born in the Iberian Peninsula were expelled from Mexico.

During the seventy-five years of the Franciscan period of the Pimería Alta, 1768–1843, the missionary college of the Holy Cross of Querétaro—mother college of the twenty-one Franciscan missionary colleges in the New World—had been the sole institution staffing the eight traditional mission districts. The expulsion of peninsular-born Spaniards in 1827–1828 decimated their ranks since most of the Querétarans had been born in Spain. The few who remained were born in Mexico. These, riding the Pimería Alta mission circuit at any one time, were usually reduced to two or three—plus two aged Spanish friars who were exempted from the expulsion due to old age or infirmity and who, for the same reason, were usually exempted from riding the challenging circuit.

On February 2, 1843, one lone friar, Father Antonio González—who in the mid-1830s had been San Xavier's last resident missionary—accompanied a group of soldiers and settlers riding south through Tubac. With his departure, the Querétarans bade a final farewell to the Pimería Alta.

The Virgin Mary in the Franciscan Churches of the Pimería Alta

Since the founding of the Franciscan Order in 1226, the Blessed Virgin has been prominent in its religious devotion. Franciscan promotion of Mary under the title of her Immaculate Conception preceded the declaration of this Marian privilege as an article of faith in the Roman Catholic Church by five hundred years. The Immaculate Conception as a dogma of faith dates only from the First Vatican Council in the middle of the nineteenth century.

The most spectacular Pimería Alta representation of the Virgin Mary is embodied in the mission church at Caborca, a structure dedicated to La Purísima Concepción de Nuestra Señora. Further visual proof of the singular rank of this devotion among Franciscans is prominent on the main altarpiece (*retablo mayor*) in the sanctuary of

Mission San Xavier del Bac. Here is a statue of Mary, her hands folded in prayer, standing on a crescent moon surrounded by clouds and angel faces, traditional testaments to her celestial connection as immortalized in an oil painting by the seventeenth century Spanish painter, Bartolomé Esteban Murillo.

The San Xavier statue is positioned on the altarpiece immediately beneath a slightly smaller sculpture of God the Father. Also of lesser dimension, at a slightly lower elevation and proportionate distance on either side of the Virgin, stand the apostles Peter and Paul, who traditionally offer stiff competition in any Roman Catholic church.

In the summer of 1841 Father Antonio González, the last of the Querétaran Franciscans to leave the Pimería Alta, recorded in a final inventory of the Mission San José de Tumacácori an image of the Immaculate Conception on the main altarpiece, though it has long since been elsewhere. The Virgin's prominent image apparently made such an impression on him that after twelve years of riding that valley and knowing well that for ninety years San José had been the popular patron of Tumacácori and all its people, Fray Antonio seems absent-mindedly to have jotted down on his assigned inventory "Purísima Concepción de Tumacácori" as the official name of the mission. There may have been a change in patronage by 1841, but if so, no other records have been found to confirm it.

Carried to Bac in 1848 by O'od-ham fleeing Apache incursions, this

lovely image from Tumacácori can now be seen in Mission San Xavier in a niche at the lowest level in the altarpiece on the north wall of the east transept. She faces a painting of the Virgin Mary as Our Lady of the Rosary which, in turn, is beneath a painting of the Virgin Mary as a child being instructed in reading by her mother, Saint Anne (*Santa Ana*), and her father, Saint Joachim (*San Joaquín*)—further evidence of the Franciscans' special devotion to Mary.

Kieran R. McCarty, O.F.M

Statue of Nuestra Señora de la Purísima Concepción, Mission San Xavier del Bac, 1995. Helga Teiwes

Left, Mission La Purísima Concepción de Nuestra Señora de Caborca, 1894. Wm. Dinwiddie

GOVERNMENT, MINING, AND AGRICULTURE

BY

JAMES E. OFFICER

In 1687, when Father Eusebio Kino established his headquarters at Dolores, the area referred to as Sonora (or Nueva Andalucía) was a province or *alcaldía mayor* within the *Reino* (Kingdom) of Nueva Vizcaya. The territory of this *Reino* consisted of the modern states of Sonora, Sinaloa, Chihuahua, and Durango, along with a portion of Coahuila. Nueva Vizcaya's governor appointed the top provincial officials, each of whom held the title *alcalde mayor*.

Sonora was much smaller then than now. The area south of the Mayo River belonged to Sinaloa, and much of the mountainous region that today makes up eastern and southeastern Sonora formed the separate jurisdiction of Ostimuri. Not until 1831, ten years after Mexico gained independence, did Sonora finally emerge as a state with a physical identity similar to its present one. The Gadsden Purchase of

Facing page: **Anza expedition leaves Tubac for California, 1775.**
Cal Peters

1854 produced the last major territorial change when an area south of the Gila River became part of the United States.

Throughout the last century of Spanish colonial rule, Sonora not only underwent territorial changes, but changes in the titles and duties of its top administrative leaders as well. So long as the area remained part of Nueva Vizcaya, these officials continued to be called *alcaldes mayores*. However, when Sonora and Sinaloa were united as an independent province in 1732, they became *gobernadores* (governors), and, after 1788, *gobernadores intendentes*. Originally, the provincial leaders had both civil and military responsibilities, but by the end of the colonial period, they exercised primarily civil powers.

When Father Kino began his work in Sonora in 1687, the capital of the province was the mining town of San Juan Bautista, the ruins of which lie today in the *municipio* (county) of Cumpas, one hundred miles south of Douglas, Arizona. In 1749 the seat of

government shifted to the *presidio* of San Miguel de Horcasitas, not far from modern Hermosillo. Arizpe, in the Sonora River Valley south of Cananea, became the colonial capital in 1777.

Before taking up his assignment in the Pimería Alta, Father Kino made it a point to pass through San Juan Bautista and pay his respects to the *alcalde mayor*. Thereafter, he cultivated close relationships with these officials and their immediate subordinates (*tenientes*, or lieutenants). Blas de Castillo, Sonora's *alcalde* in 1688, helped Kino secure the assignment of other Jesuit missionaries to the Pimería Alta, and Kino's closest companion for many of his journeys was a soldier named Juan Mateo Manje who was first a *teniente* and, later, an *alcalde mayor*.

God's Men, the King's Men, the Desert's People.

Although Kino got along well with these military men, he sometimes had problems with other soldiers. In 1688, Captain Nicolás de la Higuera and troops from Sinaloa destroyed the Pima town of Mototicachi near the headwaters of the Río Sonora. They carried some of the villagers off to Alamos to work in the mines and killed others, children among them. This behavior caused great consternation among the Indians and it appeared for a time that the entire Pimería Alta would soon be in revolt. Furthermore, the frightened European settlers began blaming the Pimas for hostile actions that were, in fact, carried out by Apaches and other tribesmen.

In 1695 Pimas in the Altar Valley mounted an insurrection that took the life of Father Francisco Xavier Saeta at Caborca. Troops brought into the area were both a help and a hindrance in getting the situation under control. Their most damaging behavior occurred during a peace conference at the village of El Tupo. Frightened that some of the Indians present might attack, the soldiers turned their guns on the Pimas, killing at least thirty who had not been involved in the uprising.

During the eighteenth century, relations between Jesuits and neighboring Spaniards were sometimes severely strained. The mission communities often included the best agricultural and grazing lands in the area, as well as the most reliable sources of water. As the Indian population declined, other settlers pressured civil and military administrators to divide the mission lands, something resisted by the priests. Also, Indians were the principal workers on the ranches and in the mines, and, to a large extent, the Jesuits controlled this labor force and opposed efforts to make greater use of it. Finally, the missionaries concentrated attention on the needs of the Indians and were sometimes reluctant or unable to perform religious services for others.

As a result of the resentment some settlers felt toward the Jesuits, civil and military administrators were quick to blame the priests for Indian uprisings such as the Yaqui Revolt of 1740 and the Pima Revolt of 1751. Influential Basque settlers of the region provided an important source of support for the missionaries during such crises. The founder of the Jesuit order, San Ignacio de Loyola, was a Basque, as was San Francisco Xavier.

Among the prominent Sonoran Basques who defended the Jesuits were Juan Bautista de Anza, father of the man credited with colonization of the San Francisco Bay area, and Bernardo de Urrea. The senior Anza commanded Spanish troops at the *presidio* of Fronteras and Urrea headed the military post at Altar. Another strong supporter was Agustín de Vildósola, governor of Sonora following the Yaqui uprising of 1740.

Many of those who came into Sonora as soldiers or civil administrators during the seventeenth and eighteenth centuries also engaged in mining and ranching. In at least one case—that of Captain Gregorio Álvarez Tuñón y Quiroz—neglect of his military responsibilities in favor of other pursuits cost him his post as commanding officer of the Fronteras *presidio*. His departure, which took place in 1725, was a source of great satisfaction to the Jesuits. For a score of years he had criticized the missionaries' resistance to exploitation of the Indian labor force.

Prospecting the Pimería Alta.

Sonora's first important mines were near the settlement of San Juan Bautista, which became the provincial capital in 1659. A quarter of a century later, important discoveries in the Sierra Madre led to the separation of that region from Sonora and it became an *alcaldía mayor* with the name of

Ostimuri. Shortly before the end of the century, the first mines in the Alamos region went into production. Kino passed through the latter area on the way to his Sonoran assignment and remarked on the quality and quantity of its mineral resources. Later, he would supply flour to the settlers there.

Contrary to popular belief, Father Kino and the other Jesuit missionaries in the Pimería Alta did not engage in mining. The precepts of their religious order specifically forbade their doing so. However, as in Kino's case, they did sell mission grain, fruit, garden produce, and livestock to residents of the mining communities. In return, they received gold and silver which they shipped to Jesuit headquarters in Mexico City. These shipments undoubtedly contributed to the popular belief that missionaries were mining and processing the ore themselves.

One of Kino's closest friends among the Sonoran miners and ranchers was Captain José Romo de Vivar, an early settler of the region and founder of the mining center of Bacanuchi a few miles northeast of Dolores. The Jesuit honored his friend by selecting Romo de Vivar as godfather for the principal chief of the Pima village of San Agustín de Oiaur, located on the Santa Cruz River within the present city limits of Tucson.

Although the Spaniards operated no mines in the Pimería Alta in Kino's day, some were engaged in ranching when the priest arrived in the region. Captain Romo de Vivar raised livestock at San Lázaro southeast of Nogales, and Juan Munguía Villela had a ranch near the modern town of Santa Cruz. Fearful of Indian attacks following the destruction of Mototicachi in 1688, both Romo de Vivar and Munguía Villela abandoned their Pimería Alta properties.

In the early eighteenth century, the first non-Indian ranching and farming communities in the Pimería Alta formed the basis for what was to become the region's permanent Hispanic population. Ranches along the Santa Cruz River between Guevavi and Santa María de Soamca, including those of San Luis, Santa Bárbara, and Buenavista, seem to have done well in the three decades between 1734 and 1764 when Apache raids made continued cattle raising there untenable.

There were also important Hispanic ranching and farming sites along the Río Magdalena between Ímuris, which had ceased to be an Indian settlement by 1801, and Santa Ana. The first of these were on the west side of the river at Santa Ana (1739) and San Lorenzo (1740). Terrenate (one of two locations in Sonora with this name) came into being early in the nineteenth century. Still in existence today, it is located between Ímuris and San Ignacio.

Despite an earlier presence of Spanish ranches in the area, the Northern Pimans did not raise livestock before the Jesuits began to work in their communities. Historians credit Father Kino with founding the cattle industry among the Indians of the Pimería Alta, although his fellow Jesuits many years earlier had brought livestock to other parts of northwestern Mexico.

The first recorded mining operations in the Pimería Alta date from the early 1720s, nearly a dozen years after Kino's death. Initially, they were concentrated in an area a few miles northeast of the mission community of Sáric. Most prominent of the early mine owners was Don Gabriel Prudhon de Bútron y Mújica, Baron of Heider, who was *alcalde mayor* of Sonora from 1727 to 1733. Arizonac was the name of his property and, in slightly modified form, it would later serve to identify an American territory and state.

In 1736, a Yaqui miner named Antonio Sirumea discovered a large sheet of nearly pure silver at a site a few miles to the northeast of Arizonac. Within a short time, other prospectors found even larger pieces, which they called *bolas* (chunks) or *planchas* (slabs) depending on their shapes. One piece, unearthed by Don José Fermín de Almazán, was reported to weigh more than a ton.

Because the mineral was so pure and lay on or near the surface, a dispute arose as to whether it was natural or processed silver. If it were processed—and, therefore, a treasure cache—it all belonged to the king. If it were natural, the king was entitled to only a share of the total value.

Juan Bautista de Anza (the elder) was Sonora's *justicia mayor* (chief justice) in 1736 and he confiscated much of the mineral pending a decision by his superiors on the question of its character. He also collected expert opinions on the matter in order to help them reach a decision. News of the discovery spread quickly and within a short time prospectors swarmed over the area.

Five years elapsed before the king of Spain finally concluded that the find was a treasure and, therefore, belonged to him. By that time, most of the silver had disappeared. Anza, who initiated the inquiry, was not around to learn of the king's decision. Apaches had slain him shortly

before at a site fifty miles east of the stream where Sirumea made his discovery and which the local settlers were already calling *Planchas de Plata*.

Mining began in southern Arizona shortly after the Planchas de Plata affair and by the middle of the eighteenth century Spaniards were extracting silver and gold from locations in the Santa Rita Mountains as well as from the Nogales and Arivaca areas. The Pima Revolt of 1751 brought an end to most of this activity. It also introduced a new round of controversy between the Jesuits and the governor of Sonora, each blaming the other for the Indian outbreak.

Native Rebellion, Jesuit Eviction, Franciscan Advent.

Another result of the Pima Revolt was the decision to establish two new *presidios* in the Pimería Alta—one at Altar and the other at Tubac. Previously the entire area had boasted only a single military post. It was located at a site on the headwaters of the San Pedro River, which at that time was called the Río Terrenate.

Late in the Jesuit period a question arose as to whether the existing *presidios* were properly organized and located for the defense of Mexico's northern

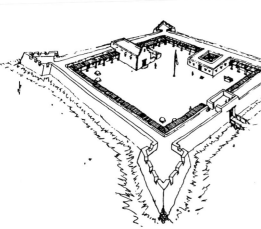

Conjectural sketch of the Tucson presidio in the late 1780s. Jack S. Williams

Conjectural sketch of the presidio of Santa Cruz de Terrenate in 1780. Jack S. Williams

50

frontier. The task of making an assessment of the situation fell to a Spanish nobleman, the Marqués de Rubí. He visited the Pimería Alta during the winter of 1766–67.

The Marqués was scarcely out of sight when King Carlos III ordered the expulsion of all Jesuits from the Spanish Empire. He thus followed in the footsteps of other absolutist rulers in nearby countries. Portugal in 1759 and France in 1764 had previously banished the Jesuits as a threat to monarchical authority.

Coronel Juan Claudio Pineda was governor of the combined provinces of Sonora and Sinaloa in 1767 when the Spanish king made his decision. In accordance with sealed instructions that he opened on July 11, Pineda called upon local military commanders to take the priests into custody and gather them at Mátape (modern Villa Pesqueira). Juan Bautista de Anza (the younger) and Bernardo Urrea, previously strong defenders of the Jesuits, were among the commanders ordered to help with the expulsion.

Urrea, *comandante* at Altar, was responsible for Pimería Alta missionaries. He assembled the Jesuits at Tubutama prior to conducting them to Mátape, where they heard for the first time the text of the king's directive. Soldiers then escorted the priests to Guay-mas, where they remained under armed guard until May 1768. Another year would elapse before any of them reached Europe. Several died along the way.

Expulsion of the Jesuits left the Indian communities and the Spanish frontier settlements without priests. In the Pimería Alta, Franciscans from Querétaro (near Mexico City) soon came to fill the gap. The first of the new missionaries arrived in the late spring of 1768. By this time, some of the earliest Jesuit missions, among them Dolores and Remedios, no longer existed.

The Franciscans concentrated their attention on the Indian communities with the greatest population. San Ignacio continued as an important center of missionary attention—along with Tubutama and Caborca. From these points, Franciscans served other nearby communities and, in a few cases, actually lived in the smaller villages.

In the final Jesuit years Guevavi had declined in both population and importance, and Tumacácori—which had never before boasted a resident priest—became Franciscan mission headquarters for the Pimans of the middle Santa Cruz River valley. San Xavier del Bac, also, received increased attention in the last quarter of the eighteenth century, as did Átil and Oquitoa in the Altar Valley.

Even the most substantial Jesuit churches and houses in the Pimería Alta were badly deteriorated when the new missionaries took over, and the Franciscans were faced with major building campaigns to replace or repair the old churches.

In January 1771, not long after the Franciscans began their work in the Pimería Alta, soldiers discovered major deposits of gold at a location south of Altar called San Ildefonso de la Cieneguilla. This find was a true bonanza and attracted hundreds of eager miners. Indians from the vicinity and from farther south, more than 1,500 of them, were among the paid laborers. At their peak, the placers of Cieneguilla produced gold that, on today's market, would be worth millions of dollars per year. The boom lasted until 1779, with another, lesser discovery coming in 1802.

Presidios and Pacification.

While Cieneguilla was the scene of frenzied activity, Juan Bautista de Anza, commanding officer of the Tubac *presidio*, made his first and second trips to Monterey and the San Francisco Bay area. During the time that he was away from his post in 1776, the

51

The Franciscan church of El Colegio Apostólico de Santa Cruz de Querétaro, México, 1995.
Bernard Fontana

little use during the remainder of the colonial period.

Viceroy Bernardo de Gálvez in the late summer of 1786 enunciated a new Indian policy that had as its aim the pacification of the northern frontier. The presidial garrisons were to be strengthened and the soldiers trained to hunt down the Indians in their strongholds and force them to sue for peace. Also, hostile tribesmen were to be encouraged to settle in camps near the *presidios* where they would be sustained through a system of rations.

Gálvez's policy led to the reestablishment of the Tubac *presidio* in 1787. During that same year, the Santa Cruz garrison moved to the old Pima town of Santa María de Soamca. The Pimería Alta thus boasted four military posts in the final years of Spanish rule. As the soldiers carried out the new policy a period of relative calm developed. More Spanish settlers moved into the area and mining and ranching again became important. With greater security from Apache depredations, the Franciscans were able to proceed with building activities in the Indian communities they served.

soldiers from his garrison at Tubac transferred their headquarters to a new *presidio* site at Tucson. Also, the troops on the upper San Pedro (Terrenate) River, moved downstream to a location called Santa Cruz a few miles northwest of the modern town of Tombstone.

It was in 1776 also that King Carlos III created a new administrative unit (*Las Provincias Internas*) for Northern Mexico. Three years later Arizpe became the capital of this unit and for a number of years thereafter was the most important center of civil and military activity in Sonora. Many prominent Mexican families living in the Pimería Alta today trace their origins to Arizpe or to the Alamos region.

Among the results of Anza's California expeditions was the decision to found missions and a Spanish town on the California side of the Colorado River near modern Yuma. In January 1781, Ensign Santiago de Islas proclaimed the official establishment of the mission of La Purísima Concepción and, a few miles upstream, the mission and town of San Pedro y San Pablo de Bicuñer. Nothing lasted long. In July, the Quechan (Yuma) Indians attacked the newcomers, killing 104, including Father Francisco Garcés and three other Franciscan friars. The Spaniards would attempt no more settlements in this area and Anza's California trail would see

The Mexican independence movement began in 1810, and while none of the fighting took place in the Pimería Alta, soldiers from all the garrisons in the area went south to defend the Spanish crown. Some were still on detached service as late as 1818. The time they spent away from their homes and families counted as double toward their retirement.

Between 1821 and the Gadsden Purchase of 1854, the towns of the Pimería Alta were largely neglected by the central government in Mexico City and left to their own devices. Apache attacks increased and led to the abandonment of many frontier villages, mines, and missions.

After 1843, The missionaries were gone and most of the communities in the Pimería Alta received only occasional visits from secular priests stationed at San Ignacio and Altar and from the military chaplain at Santa Cruz. When the Gadsden Purchase brought a portion of the area under United States control in 1854, the majority of the Spanish mission churches of the area were badly deteriorated or in ruins. Some would never be used again.

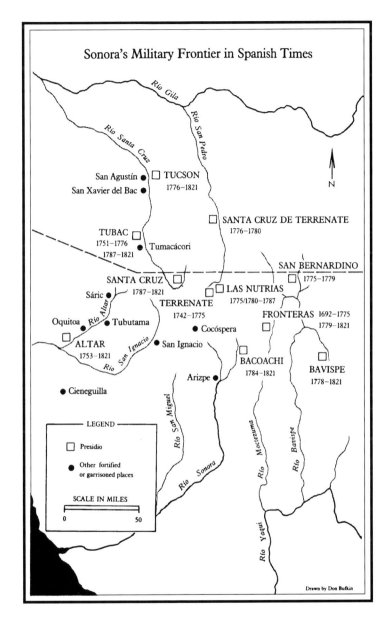

Sonora's Military Frontier in Spanish Times

Río Gila

Río Santa Cruz

Río San Pedro

San Agustín ● □ TUCSON
1776–1821
San Xavier del Bac ●

□ SANTA CRUZ DE TERRENATE
1776–1780

TUBAC □
1751–1776
1787–1821
● Tumacácori

SAN BERNARDINO
□ 1775–1779

SANTA CRUZ □
Sáric ● 1787–1821
□ LAS NUTRIAS
1775/1780–1787
TERRENATE
1742–1775
FRONTERAS 1692–1775
□ 1779–1821

Oquitoa ● Río Altar ● Tubutama
● Cocóspera

ALTAR
1753–1821
Río San Ignacio ● San Ignacio
BACOACHI
1784–1821
BAVISPE
1778–1821

● Cieneguilla
Arizpe ●

LEGEND

□ Presidio

● Other fortified
or garrisoned places

SCALE IN MILES
0   50

Río San Miguel

Río Sonora

Río Moctezuma

Río Bavispe

Río Yaqui

Drawn by Don Bufkin

THE COLUMBIAN EXCHANGE

BY

THOMAS E. SHERIDAN

In March 1699, Father Eusebio Kino, Father Adam Gilg, and Captain Juan Mateo Manje visited six O'odham settlements in the Tucson Basin. For Kino and Manje, it was their fifth expedition together. A faithful journal keeper, the young lieutenant of the *alcalde mayor* described how the Pimans received the three Europeans with arches, crosses, and gifts of food. Then he wrote

The natives were given a long talk on our holy Catholic faith, and also on the obedience and subjection they were required to pledge to the king. Secondarily, they were called upon to unite themselves with all the Pimería by warring against the enemy Jocomes and Apaches, who overrun the Spaniards of the province of Sonora with their repeated murders and thefts of livestock. The Pimas responded that they would confer on this matter and leave to join in the war. Furthermore, they said that the people of Captain Humari—the chief of those who live along the Terrenate (San Pedro) River twenty-five leagues east of here, near

Facing page: **cattle on the ranch of Carlos Vanegas south of Pitiquito, 1988.** Bernard Fontana

the enemy nations that also do them harm—had just finished destroying a rancheria of Apaches, capturing some children and other booty.[2]

This was in response to an Apache attack on the pueblo of Santa María de Soamca three weeks earlier, when the enemies ran off the few horses the community had. The people of Humari had gone forth to avenge that raid, just as the Pimans would do now.

The Incongruity of Conquest.

Read in the light of later developments, Manje's terse remarks are a text that captures many of the contradictions that characterized Spain's attempt to conquer the Pimería Alta. Kino and Manje represented *Las Ambas Majestades* (Both Majesties)—God and the king—the twin pillars of the Spanish Empire. They may have come in peace, without a military escort, but they also wanted to shake the very foundations of Piman society. Their world was a world of rigid hierarchies and

dichotomies—salvation or damnation, faith or apostasy, subjection or treason. By missionizing the O'odham, Kino and Manje hoped to draw them into the empire and trigger a political revolution that would carry the empire across the Pimería Alta to the Gila River and beyond. Missionization was an imperial endeavor as well as a religious conversion.

Yet even as they delivered their orations, events had escalated beyond their control. Kino and Manje wanted to turn pagans into Christians, desert-dwellers into town-dwellers, and free men and women into vassals, but many of the transformations they unleashed were unintended and unforeseen. In the final analysis, seeds, genes, and microbes changed more lives than Catholic doctrine or Spanish imperial designs. What historian Alfred Crosby calls the Columbian Exchange—that interchange of plants, animals, and other organisms between Europe and the Americas—was already flowing across the Pimería Alta like lava, rearranging the cultural topography in its wake.

A case in point was the Apache raid on Santa María and Humari's response. When Columbus crossed the Atlantic in 1492, the Americas (the New World) had been isolated from Eurasia and Africa (the Old World) for more than twelve thousand years after the Bering land bridge disappeared beneath the sea. During those millennia, people in both worlds learned how to cultivate plants and settle in villages and cities. But one crucial difference emerged. The people of Eurasia domesticated cattle, horses, sheep, and goats. The people of North America domesticated only turkeys and dogs. Horses did not exist in the Pimería Alta until the Europeans arrived, and were perhaps the most valuable currency of the Columbian Exchange. The Apaches attacked Santa María to steal horses given to O'odham by Kino and other missionaries.

And Santa María merely marked an initial skirmish. Manje's account describes the origins of a pattern of guerrilla warfare that dominated the history of the Pimería Alta for the next two hundred years. The Apaches would attack, the Spaniards and O'odham would give pursuit, both sides murdering adults and taking children captive whenever possible. It was a bloody cycle of provocation and revenge, and it did not end until Geronimo surrendered to General Nelson Miles in 1886, long after both the Spanish Empire and the Jesuit mission system had collapsed.

The introduction of Old World livestock may have given the O'odham draft animals to pull their plows and beef, mutton, and dairy products to enrich their diet, but those same animals made them a target of Apache raids. By 1762, Humari's descendants had been forced to abandon the San Pedro River Valley and move to settlements along the Santa Cruz and elsewhere. By the early 1800s, Pimas living on the Gila River had developed what amounted to a standing army of a thousand men—nearly one-fourth of their total population. The O'odham paid a heavy price for Kino's largesse.

Cultural Exchange and Contagion.

The domestication of livestock brought about another difference between the Old and New Worlds as well. Eurasian peoples grew up with horses, cattle, sheep, goats, hogs, and domestic fowls. As they did, many diseases afflicting animals jumped from animal to human hosts and back again, triggering cycles of infection and mutation that produced smallpox and cowpox, measles, distemper, rinderpest, and many different strains of influenza. These pestilences swept through Old World populations in terrible epidemics that exterminated millions. Over the generations, however, the so-called childhood diseases became endemic rather than epidemic, killing only a small percentage of the population but rarely threatening the fabric of society itself. But the people of the New World had little or no exposure to smallpox, measles, influenza, and malaria before 1492. Once the genetic insularity of the Americas was breached, epidemics spread with terrifying rapidity. In many parts of the New World, Indian populations declined by an estimated 80 to 95 percent during the first 150 years of contact.

The first great pandemic of smallpox in North America began in 1521 when a soldier accompanying the expedition from Cuba to arrest Hernán Cortez unleashed the virus upon Mesoamerica's resistance-free populations. The pandemic decimated the Aztec and Tarascan empires, and by 1525 it was ravaging the Incas of South America as well. But whether or not it or any of the other sixteenth-century pandemics of smallpox, measles, typhus, or

Horse Culture in the Pimería Alta

The history of New Spain would have been far different without horses. It was primarily horses that arrived with Cortez's soldiers in 1519 that gave Spaniards the advantage over hosts of native warriors who confronted them on their advance to the Valley of Mexico. It was horses that permitted the opening up of the arid northern lands to cattle raising. And it was horses that gave the Apaches the great mobility that enabled them to halt the flow of Spanish empire on the edges of their territory.

Horses and cattle go together, especially in the wide spaces of northern Mexico. The techniques that Spanish and, later, Mexican *vaqueros* evolved for working cattle in open range—roping, roundups, and the lot—were borrowed wholesale in the late nineteenth century by American cowboys. Even the jargon of the cowboy had its origins in New Spain: *jáquima* became hackamore; *mecate*, or horsehair rope, became McCarty; *la reata*, the braided rawhide catch-rope, became a lariat; *mesteño* was anglicized to mustang; and a *vaquero* became a buckaroo.

The Pimería Alta has been horse and cattle country ever since Father Kino rode north of the Rim of Christendom in 1687. Beef and cheese remain staples in the Sonoran diet of

the 1990s. In fact, José Vasconcelos, an intellectual and political figure of the Mexican Revolution, is said to have referred to Sonora as the place "where civilization ends and *carne asada* (charbroiled beef) begins."

Men in northern Sonora still work cattle from horseback, roping, branding, and employing all the skills of the traditional vaquero. Many of the old crafts are still pursued as well. I once noticed a man crouched by a fresh cowhide on the ground. I stopped for a visit and discovered that his cow had been hit and killed by a truck a few hours before. He had skinned her out and was cutting her hide into thin strips with which to braid a *reata*, or lariat. This is a thrifty

country where everything has its use and people still know how to "make something out of nothing."

But life isn't all work, and even hard-working cattlemen must play once in awhile. When Sonoran ranch folk get together on a fiesta day, they often have horse races. More specifically, they hold match races, pitting two horses against each other. In the old days, they were simply fast ranch horses. Now ranchers purchase race horses especially for these events, and one can often see such beautiful steeds being exercised on a Saturday morning at Santa Ana Viejo and other ranching communities.

Most traditional singers know at least one or two *corridos* about famous horses or the races they ran. Especially popular is *"El Moro de Cumpas,"* that tells about a race that took place in Agua Prieta, Sonora, in 1957.

James S. Griffith

dysentery reached the Pimería Alta remains to be determined. Anthropologists Henry Dobyns and Daniel Reff believe that the great prehistoric Hohokam civilization of central and southern Arizona collapsed because of such epidemics, which preceded the arrival of Spanish missionaries and settlers by traveling along Indian trade routes. Most archaeologists, on the other hand, contend that the Hohokam disappeared during the 1400s before the spread of Old World microbes. It is a difficult question to resolve, because Hohokam chronology is imprecise and diseases like smallpox leave no signatures on bones. The O'odham Kino encountered may have been descendants of the Hohokam living simpler lives. Or they may have been relative newcomers to the Pimería Alta, moving into a depopulated frontier. We may never know the answer.

We do know this, however: once European missionaries and Spanish colonists settled among the O'odham, Old World diseases took a terrible toll. Nuestra Señora de los Remedios (ironically, Our Lady of Remedies) was abandoned because of disease and Apache attacks in the 1730s. Kino's mission headquarters of Dolores met the same fate the following decade. The mission communities

of the west along the Magdalena, Altar, and Concepción Rivers weathered the expulsion of the Jesuits in 1767 and Mexican independence in 1821. But as Piman populations declined and more and more Spaniards moved into the region, settlements such as Caborca, Magdalena, and Tubutama began to lose their identities as O'odham communities. By the twentieth century, O'odham made up a very small percentage of the inhabitants of those riverine towns.

Even the mission communities that survived were unable to reproduce themselves. At San Xavier del Bac, for example, the Piman population continually dwindled. The only way Bac persevered as an O'odham community was by augmenting its numbers with Sobaípuri Pimas from the San Pedro River or Papagos from the western deserts. It is easy to understand why so many O'odham came to hate the Europeans and to associate the tolling of church bells with the spread of disease and death. The Spaniards did not deliberately try to infect the O'odham, but the unforeseen consequences of their conquest were more devastating than the repression of any Pima rebellion.

It is interesting to speculate about the psychological impact of Old World diseases upon the

O'odham. On the one hand, fear of contagion undoubtedly drove many Pimans to resists missionization and to flee the Europeans. On the other, the relative immunity of the Europeans must have increased their prestige in O'odham eyes. Pimans believed that powerful medicine men known as *mámakai* had the ability to diagnose and cure disease. They also believed that some individuals could cause disease. Modern O'odham draw a distinction between "staying" sicknesses, which afflict only Pimans, and "wandering" sicknesses that affect all humanity. That distinction may have originated during the mission period, when epidemics of smallpox and measles "wandered" from one community to another. O'odham may also have regarded the missionaries as *mámakai* who communicated with new supernaturals—*Cristo, la Virgen María, San Francisco*—and had the power to inflict disease and death. No wonder O'odham attitudes toward the Europeans were so ambivalent, veering between alliance and rebellion.

Cultural Exchange and Native Choices.

Some European introductions sustained rather than destroyed. The O'odham were sophisticated desert farmers who grew many varieties of corn, beans, and squash adapted to their arid climate, yet none of their major food crops could survive hard frosts. That meant that Pimans living in the Tucson Basin and other upland areas of the Sonoran Desert could not cultivate their fields from November through March, when frosts were a danger. When Kino and his companions established missions among the O'odham, however, they gave them gifts of seeds and nursery stock as well as animals, more than doubling the number of cultigens available to Piman farmers. Lentils, chickpeas (garbanzos), fava beans, cabbage, onions, leeks, garlic, cowpeas, sugar cane, mustard, anise, mint, pepper, melons, apples, grapes, quinces, peaches, plums, pomegranates, apricots, figs—thousands of years of Old World agricultural experience and experimentation—were suddenly placed in O'odham hands.

The most important introduction was winter wheat. First cultivated in the neolithic Near East, wheat flourished during months when corn and beans would have shriveled from the cold. It therefore filled a gap in the Piman agricultural cycle, allowing the O'odham to farm year round. Wheat also enabled some O'odham, especially those along the Gila River, to live in larger, more compact villages, an important defensive measure as Apache raiding intensified during the eighteenth and nineteenth centuries. Beginning in the 1840s, Pimans on the Gila even became Arizona's first agricultural entrepreneurs, selling or trading wheat flour and other produce to thousands of European American soldiers, forty-niners, and other travelers along the famous Gila Trail to California. By 1870, the O'odham were selling more than three million pounds of wheat. If Anglo and Mexican farmers upstream had not diverted their water and dried up their fields, O'odham, not Anglos, might have made Phoenix rise from the ashes of the Hohokam.

Kino and Manje had their own agendas when they rode into the Pimería Alta. Among some of the O'odham, they succeeded. Among others, their goals fell victim to chance, circumstance, and the agendas of Pimans themselves. The O'odham brought their own goals and desires to the chessboard we call Spanish colonial history. Even in situations where the Spaniards held the balance of power, Pimans chose what symbols and commodities to incorporate into their own society and culture. They enthusiastically accepted wheat, cattle, and horses. They selectively accepted certain Christian rituals and beliefs. In 1695 and 1751, some of them violently rejected Spanish civil authority or mission discipline.

Their rejection might have been more sustained if not for the Western Apaches, who brought the O'odham and the Spaniards together in a way missionization never could. The Akimel O'odham of the Gila River and the Tohono O'odham of the western deserts never supported missionaries among them, yet they fought alongside Spanish and later Mexican soldiers for nearly two hundred years. In the end, their bonds were those of bloodshed more than faith, ties of necessity rather than a shared sense of mission community. That was not the vision Kino and Manje carried with them when they passed through the Pimería Alta. And what that should teach us whenever we attempt to change another people is that we are never completely the masters of our own destinies, that no matter how good or bad our intentions may be, our impact upon others may take trajectories we can neither foresee nor control.

MISSION CHURCHES OF NORTHERN SONORA

BY
MARDITH SCHUETZ-MILLER
AND
BERNARD L. FONTANA

The mission churches of the Pimería Alta were late blossoms on an ornamental tree whose roots, trunk, and branches lay in the Near East, North Africa, Spain, and farther south in Mexico (New Spain). To appreciate the architecture of these churches requires at least some understanding of the larger setting, both geographic and historical, out of which it grew.

Missionary presence in Sonora preceded Father Kino's arrival in the Pimería Alta by nearly 150 years. Franciscan priests were members of the earliest Spanish expeditions passing through the region in the 1500s. It was only in 1687, however, when Father Kino crossed the Rim of Christendom, that the northern O'odham began to feel the full impact of the mission program.

Spanish settlement of Sonora began officially in 1640 when the presidial commander of the Villa

Facing page: **Ceiling detail from Mission Nuestra Señora de Asunción de Arizpe, 1957.** James Officer

de Sinaloa, Don Pedro de Perea, was named *alcalde mayor* of the newly created province of Nueva Andalucía (Sonora). In 1641 Perea established several small ranching communities, including his own Hacienda Nombre de Dios, in the Sonora River Valley. Three years later he recruited additional colonists and five Franciscan priests from New Mexico. Some of the New Mexican friars had visited briefly in the Bavispe and Sonora river valleys in 1632 and again in 1638.

For five or six years Franciscans labored with indifferent success—labors which in 1645 included at least one *entrada* as far west as the "Cipia" (O'odham) village of Hímeris (Ímuris) in what was eventually to be known as the Pimería Alta—and squabbled with the Jesuits who considered Sonora to be their mission jurisdiction. In 1650 the two religious orders

signed a formal agreement which established the mountains east of the Río Bavispe as the dividing line between Jesuit territory on the west and Franciscan territory on the east. Subsequently, in 1653, the Jesuits began to establish their first permanent missions in the region.[3]

There is a distinction between a mission and a church. In its primary sense, the term mission applies to the act of missionizing, to the activity with which a group of missionaries is charged. It is only secondarily that mission refers to a building or compound. The latter is more properly a

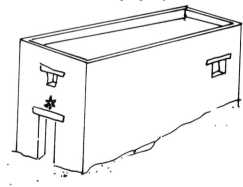

The rectangular, hall-shaped adobe church of the Jesuits in the Pimería Alta.

church, a structure within whose confines religious services are conducted. When the Jesuit priests established a mission in a community, it meant they began their work of proselytizing—with or without a building. Indeed, the first so-called churches were generally little more than ramadas, roofed shelters supported by four corner posts and without walls.

Jesuit Churches.

The earliest Jesuit churches in Sonora that went beyond simple shelters were built with materials readily at hand: adobe, small timbers, and river boulders, their simplicity a mirror of the lack of sophistication among available workers even as they signalled expediency. Almost springing from the earth on which they stood, these buildings reflected the economic and environmental realities of the region. Their basic component, the mold-made, sun-dried adobe brick, was a European introduction in this part of the New World, an element ultimately traceable to origins in Middle Eastern architecture.

Such rectangular, hall-shaped adobe churches were of a form immediately rooted in Islamic/ Gothic, or *mudéjar*, beginnings in the Iberian peninsula. These buildings had flat, wood roofs characterized by the use of wooden beams (*vigas*) supported on corbels (*zapatas*) resting on the tops of walls and covered at right angles with lathes (*latillas*) of cane, willow, saguaro ribs, or similar material sealed with mud, grass or straw, cow manure, and, rarely, lime mortar. These kinds of temples, which included simply adorned facades, were typical of those found in lower Andalucía. The diffusion of such a practical model to the New World was almost an inevitability.

The interior of a hall church often featured an arch to mark the separation between nave and sanctuary. Frequently, the sanctuary was raised in elevation above the nave as a further means of dividing these functional areas.

Flat-roofed, sun-dried adobe buildings required constant maintenance lest they quickly deteriorate. However, frontier conditions made it necessary to use such perishable elements. For example, timber suitable for construction near mission establishments was scarce. Large trees had to be brought from the mountains to the east at a time when there were no proper roads and when Apaches were a threat to life and limb. Jesuit missionaries commented on the availability of good stone and materials for manufacturing lime and mortar if masons and stone-cutters could be found willing to come to the frontier. But there was scant possibility of that since there was no hope of monetary gain in a province where few Spaniards could afford such services and the Indians had no need of them since they could erect their own circular brush huts in a day's time.[4]

Such hall churches continued to be constructed in Sonora under Jesuit direction virtually up to the time of their expulsion in 1767. The simplicity of these earliest houses of worship found some compensation in beautiful altars, paintings, statuary, and other adornments brought from Mexico City[5] or in embellishments by local artisans.

An exemplar of the local artisan is Francisco Pintor Monte, a Lower Pima (southern O'odham) from Ures whom Father Kino brought with him to the Pimería Alta as an interpreter, catechist, and native governor for his headquarters mission of Nuestra Señora de los Dolores. Francisco, known as El Pintor, accompanied Father Kino and his soldier traveling companion Juan Mateo Manje on four of their major exploratory expeditions to the Papaguería and elsewhere in the Pimería Alta between 1697 and 1701. The multi-talented Pintor, as his name suggests, was a painter as well, and during a 1701 trip with Kino in search of an overland route to California, he whitewashed and decorated an adobe chapel which the O'odham had erected at San Marcelo de Sonoyta, a far western *visita* of Caborca.[6]

The example illustrates another practice in the mission-ization process: that of bringing converts to new mission stations as assistants in teaching neophytes the Catholic doctrine, the Castilian language, and European skills. If Father Juan Nentvig was correct, the Pimans were particularly recep-tive to learning new techniques. He wrote of them: "Along certain lines the Indian's application and natural ability make him proficient, for example, in playing musical instruments, carpentering, black-smithing, stone-cutting, and even house-building."[7] The O'odham of Caborca undoubtedly got their first instruction in western build-ing techniques when Father Kino brought carpenters, possibly Opata Indians, there in 1706 to help finish the first church.[8]

By the first half of the eight-eenth century, a few of the older Jesuit missions in northern Sonora began to reflect a stability achieved through almost a half century of proselytizing among the resident Lower Pimas, Opatas, and Jovas and through the inexorable colo-nization of the area by Spaniards.

A handful of more permanent churches replaced the earlier adobe buildings.

Among the latter was San Miguel Arcángel de Oposura (today's Moctezuma), located on the Río Moctezuma. The large burnt brick church with vaulted ceiling, side bays, and an octagonal chapel with a wooden roof was built by unidentified *maestros* brought to the site at great expense by Father Daniel Janusque sometime before his death in 1724. It continued under two of his successors until it was finished in February 1738.[9] Oposura was secularized following the Jesuit expulsion and never became a Franciscan mission.

Another permanent church was San Francisco Xavier de Batuc, also in the valley of the Río Moctezuma. It was begun under the auspices of Father Alejandro Rapicani in the late 1750s. To construct this neo-classic building of cut limestone with its vaulted roof he engaged a mason/ architect, whose name remains unknown, from Mexico City who, with the help of local Eudebe Indians whom he trained, erected the edifice in short order.[10] Before this handsome temple was inun-dated beneath the waters behind El Novillo Dam in 1964, the facade was dismantled and reassembled in a park south of downtown Her-

mosillo. The simple, but elegant, gateway to the mission's cemetery was re-erected opposite the historic mission at Caborca where it has become a favorite frame through which photographers can capture an image of the front of that early nineteenth-century structure.[11]

Father Salvador de la Peña, who was at Cucurpe between about 1750 and 1763, replaced his deteriorating house with one of cut stone with the help of some Indians and "a poor Spaniard who was nothing more than a bungler of the art of masonry." Lacking the ability to construct arches, the house was finished with a flat "Mexican style" roof of fired bricks laid over the *vigas* and sealed with a three or four-inch layer of mortar. The mortar was levelled and burnished to the point that "such a roof is incomparable for protecting the building even from continuous rains,"[12] cause enough to question the indictment of the local builder as a "bungler."

Contemporary with the mission church at Batuc was one of fired brick, stone, and lime mortar erected by the Jesuits at Arizpe. Its patroness is Nuestra Señora de la Asunción and con-struction began in the 1740s or perhaps slightly earlier. It was dedicated more or less in its present form in 1756 during the administration of Father Carlos

Mission Nuestra Señora de la Asunción de Arizpe, 1984.

Bernard Fontana

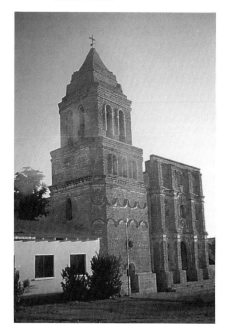

Rojas, who was at Arizpe from 1727 until the Jesuit expulsion in 1767. The church has fired brick walls with stone rubble cores and is one of few such structures with a separate bell tower ever erected on the northern frontier. (Another is a few miles south at Sinoquipe where the tower remains some distance from what little is left of the original fabric of the chapel). The Arizpe tower, built in three tiers, was never finished with a cupola in colonial times. The pyramid which caps it today was added sometime between 1879 and 1910.[13]

In the immediate aftermath of the Jesuit expulsion, Arizpe was turned over in 1768 to blue-robed friars from the Franciscan Province of Santiago de Jalisco, with Fray Juan Domínguez drawing the assignment, one which occupied him until 1780 when he was replaced by secular priest Miguel Elías González.[14]

Pope Pius VI established the Diocese of Sonora (including Sinaloa) in May 1779, anticipating that the headquarters would be in Arizpe which a short time before had been designated as the capital of the Provincias Internas. However, Antonio de los Reyes, Sonora's first bishop, chose to reside in Alamos. In September 1783 he obtained the endorsement of Felipe de Neve, governor and general commander of the Provincias Internas, to a letter he sent to the archbishop in Mexico City and to the Council of the Indies expressing his wishes concerning transfer of the diocesan headquarters from Arizpe to Alamos.[15]

Although technically the church of Nuestra Señora de la Asunción de Arizpe might be regarded as having had the status of a cathedral when the diocese was created, neither Reyes nor any of his successors ever lived in the town. Furthermore, the headquarters of the Sonora bishopric moved to Culiacán in 1799 and

remained there for nearly a hundred years.[16]

Given the sumptuousness of Jesuit constructions where conditions permitted, there should be little doubt that the simpler adobes would have been replaced in the Pimería Alta as elsewhere with more durable structures had it not been for the expulsion of members of the society in 1767.

When Father Kino arrived in the Pimería Alta in 1687 he first established Nuestra Señora de los Dolores as his home base and immediately started founding a chain of missions in spite of the fact that he was aided by only three other missionaries for the initial five years. By 1694 he had begun missions among existing O'odham settlements almost as far north as the Arizona border, and he had bestowed saints' names on villages north of the border. Cattle herds, fields of grain, and orchards flourished at Dolores, Cocóspera, San Ignacio, and Tubutama and another mission and *visita* had been started at Caborca and Pitiquito, respectively. Before he died in 1711, Kino had extended his mission complex into Arizona with San Gabriel de Guevavi, San Cayetano de Tumacácori, San Xavier del Bac, and lesser stations.

The number of *cabeceras*, churches with resident priests, and *visitas*, Indian settlements served by circuit-riding padres from *cabeceras*, varied from year to year. All fell victim at one time or another to destruction at the hands of hostile tribes, rebellion among those for whom they had been established, desertion, or simply from deterioration due to a dearth of missionaries.

Franciscan Inheritance.

Franciscans from the Apostolic College of the Holy Cross of Querétaro took over the Pimería Alta missions in 1768. Out of fifteen Sonoran missions with their *visitas* shouldered that year by the gray-robed friars from Querétaro, eight were located in the Pimería Alta: San Xavier del Bac (with the *visita* of San Agustín del Tucson); Los Santos Ángeles de Guevavi (with *visitas* at San Ignacio de Sonoitac, San José de Tumacácori, and San Cayetano de Calabazas); Santa María de Soamca (with a *visita* at Nuestra Señora del Pilar y Santiago de Cocóspera); San Ignacio de Cabórica (with *visitas* at San José de Ímuris and Santa María Magdalena); Nuestra Señora de los Dolores del Sáric (with a *visita* at San José de Aquimuri); San Pedro y San Pablo de Tubutama (with a *visita* at Santa Teresa); San Francisco de Átil (and its *visita* of San Antonio Paduano del

Oquitoa); and, finally, La Purísima Concepción de Nuestra Señora de Caborca (with *visitas* at San Diego de Pitiquito and Santa María del Pópulo de Bísanig).[17]

The Franciscan who arrived at Santa María de Soamca in June 1768 and his O'odham neophytes abandoned the mission in November in the wake of an Apache attack and occupied Cocóspera instead.[18]

The adobe structures in Sonora inherited from the Jesuits by the Franciscans were generally in a bad state of repair. Matters were made worse by the fact that between the time the Jesuits departed in 1767 and the Franciscans arrived in 1768, and for a year afterward, what had formerly been such mission properties as livestock, farmlands, and agricultural products were turned over to civil commissioners. Franciscans were left with only their residences, churches, and their effects. Unlike the Jesuits, they had no right to products of Indians' labor and were expected to get along solely with the annual stipend from the royal treasury. Even furnishings and repairs to buildings were supposed to come out of their skimpy royal salary.

Although perhaps an extreme example, the story of the church taken over by the Franciscans at Ures in Sonora's Pimería Baja

provides insight into conditions confronted by the friars:

The church at Mission San Miguel de los Ures had been the pride of the Pimerías in the Jesuit days. The Marqués de Rubí frontier inspection team had been in Ures on February 23, 1767. Nicolás de Lafora, chronicler of the expedition and captain of the Royal Spanish Engineers, described the church: "In its architecture and church ornaments it excels all other missions." (Father) Salazar had been at Ures a little over two months when the pride of the Pimerías became so unsafe that he had to close it. On Saint Dominic's Day, August 4, 1768, two of the main beams supporting the ceiling came crashing to the floor minutes before Mass was to begin. Miraculously, no one was injured. Salazar moved the altar out and built a primitive ramada over it. The Spanish mission at Ures was starting all over again. He reported on the condition of the sacristy. The beams were rotten, the roof leaking, and the old adobes washing away. . . . Salazar resorted to irony when he hoped the Indians would feel freer hearing Mass in the open, since freedom was their strongest passion and especially since pollparrot, he thought, would become king before the church could be repaired under the (civil commissioner) system of 1768. He resigned himself to standing by and watching the church crumble to the ground, piece by piece.[19]

In 1772, Father Antonio María de los Reyes, who eight

years later became the first Bishop of Sonora, penned a lengthy report concerning the missions of Sonora then under the administration of the friars of the College of the Holy Cross at Querétaro. Father Reyes seems never to have visited the Pimería Alta, and for that part of his report he was forced to rely on hearsay and whatever records were available to him. Nonetheless, his descriptions of Pimería Alta churches and houses at that early date of their administration by Franciscans are instructive, although they cannot be accepted uncritically.

Even though the civil commissioner system was terminated in 1769 and control of all mission properties had been returned to the missionaries, Father Reyes's report makes it clear there had been little building progress by 1772. He wrote that all the churches and houses of the missionaries were of adobe and roofed with wood, grass, and earth. A few Indians—and they were the exception—also had adobe houses.[20]

In spite of the many difficulties, however, including serious attacks by Apaches, Seris, and unconverted and apostate O'odham in 1776 as well as at other times, a Franciscan building program got underway in the Pimería Alta beginning in the decade of the 1770s. In 1793, Fray Francisco Antonio Barbastro, former Father President of the Missions of Pimería Alta, penned an unabashedly enthusiastic report on the state of affairs:

In all the pueblos and missions the churches are respectable and the sacristies are provided with all the vestments and sacred vessels. In all of them ecclesiastical functions are carried out with the same order and rituals ordered by our Mother the Church in the rest of the Christian world. During the time that my college (of Holy Cross of Querétaro) has governed these missions they introduced the use of lime mortar and brick with which the Indians were previously unacquainted, and with these materials they raised from the foundations the churches of Piti-qui(to), San Ignacio, Sáric, and Tubutama, always keeping the sword in one hand to fight the enemy and the trowel in the other. They constructed them with the most beautiful arches which, like something never before seen, caused admiration not only in the Pimería but in all of Sonora and roused the praises of God. All of them have been praised, and at last we hope to see finished this year (1793–94) the church which they are building in the Mission of San Xavier del Bac. That is the northernmost pueblo of the Christian world and everyone thinks it rivals the most beautiful churches in Mexico. In this country it should rightly be termed "astounding."[21]

By piecing together various accounts, it becomes possible to summarize the history of construction of those early Pimería Alta churches which remain standing.

San Pedro y San Pablo del Tubutama

Because this was the headquarters of religious administration for the entire Pimería Alta during much of the Jesuit and Franciscan periods, it can be argued that after 1732, at least, it was also the most important church, the very hub of Pimería Alta mission activities. It is where Father Jacobo Sedelmayr, head of the Jesuit province of Pimería Alta, was stationed at the outbreak of the Pima Rebellion of 1751; it is where Jesuits gathered in 1767 for their expulsion; it is where Franciscans established their Pimería Alta headquarters in 1768; and it is where in 1776–77 Franciscan friars Francisco Garcés and Pedro Font cloistered themselves to write their lengthy accounts of their involvement in the 1775–76 overland colonizing expedition to Alta California led by Juan Bautista de Anza.[22]

Established by the Jesuits in 1691, the first mission building at Tubutama may have been destroyed in the Pima uprising of 1695. A second adobe church was completed in 1699 and a third may have been finished in 1706. Construction on a successor had been started in 1730 and a fifth, built of more than fifty thousand adobes, was underway in 1747 only to be destroyed in the Pima Rebellion of 1751. A diorama in the museum at Tumacacori National Historical Park in Arizona depicts the scene of the 1751 Tubutama conflagration.

While the 1751 rebellion had reduced Jesuit missionary Jacobo Sedelmayr's house of worship to ashes, Father Luis Vivas, his successor in 1753, was able to build a new adobe church by 1764, one with two altars, a small side chapel, and a sacristy. The first Franciscan to reside there in 1768 begged that the civil commissioner give him some old cloaks and pieces of heavy Chinese linen left

Mission San Pedro y San Pablo del Tubutama, 1990. James Officer

by the Jesuits so he could cover the windows of the building to keep out the bats. This was not a very impressive *cabecera* whose downstream *visita* of Santa Teresa was probably even less well off.[21]

As at San Xavier del Bac and elsewhere, in the second half of the 1770s the Franciscans went to work to build a more substantial temple for Tubutama. In 1793, reporting from his mission station at Aconchi on the Sonora River, Father Antonio Barbastro, who served at Tubutama from 1776 to 1783, reminisced

. . . For eight years I was a missionary in the Pimería Alta at Tubutama, which has only eight families and is continually being harassed by the Apaches.

Main entrance to the mission, Tubutama, 1925. George Boundey

On various occasions I saw the enemy as close as the place where our women drew the water. On two occasions they stole the village oxen. On another two occasions they stole all the village livestock. Some of our village Indians they killed; others they took captive. They killed my missionary companion, Fray Felipe Guillén (in 1778). And yet, after clothing my village Indians, giving gifts to the Papagos (from the desert), and all the other ordinary expenses, I was able to build a church some eighty-two feet long and over sixteen feet wide, with a transept, a dome-shaped cupola above, and a famous facade. From the foundations everything was brick and lime plaster. On dedication day (in 1783) we featured eleven statues and a (liturgical) lamp all of silver.[24]

We know from other sources that Barbastro's successor, Francisco Yturralde, who remained at Tubutama until 1799, also had a hand in the building's construction. Both physical evidence and documentary records suggest that the baptistery, with its *mudéjar* arched entrance, was an Yturralde addition made before 1796.[25]

Tubutama was perhaps the first settlement in the Pimería Alta laid out as a fortified town with the houses built into the ramparts and their doors opening onto the plaza. The walls had only two narrow gates which were closed sundown to sunrise to protect the people and oxen enclosed inside at

Main altarpiece, Tubutama church, 1978. John Schaefer

The outskirts of Tubutama, ca. 1940. Edward Ronstadt

night. Father Barbastro wrote: "At dawn, which is the most dangerous time, I ordered them to ring the seven (church) bells and to keep it up till the sun rose. The people and their cattle did not leave the village until the sun was quite high and the whole mission had been fortified. There were three guns with enough powder and balls."[26]

The interior of Tubutama's church is especially noteworthy for a transept dedicated to the Passion of Christ and which has sculptured in plaster in bas-relief on its altarpiece instruments of the Passion: crown of thorns, scourge, nails, tongs, ladder, and lances. A sculptured serpent crawls beneath an upper niche in the same altarpiece. This recess now holds a carved statue of Our Lady of Aránzazu, an image of the Virgin Mary as she appeared at Aránzazu in the Basque country of northern Spain. Oral tradition holds that the statue was originally in the chapel in Tubutama's downstream *visita* of Santa Teresa, now an adobe ruin. Given the large numbers of Basques who played key roles in the viceregal period of Sonoran history (Juan Bautista de Anza, for example, was a Basque), it is not surprising Our Lady of Aránzazu should have found her way here.

The early eighteenth-century carved-wood main altarpiece,

which features five oil paintings depicting scenes in the life of San José (Saint Joseph), is obviously one originally intended for use in a church dedicated to San José rather to San Pedro y San Pablo (saints Peter and Paul). There is a possibility it may once have adorned the post-1751 Jesuit edifice at San José de Tumacácori, or, less likely, it may have been in the interior of the Jesuit chapel at San José de Ímuris. It may also have been sent to the Pimería as a donation by a more affluent congregation farther to the south, a parish whose clergy and flock may have regarded it as being out of style and therefore worthy of a needy mission on the frontier.

Other unusual decorative elements in Tubutama are the carved wooden pomegranates pendant from the ceiling beneath the choir loft.

Visitors are charmed by the bas-relief sculptures on the building's facade. Not only is there a sun dial here, but so is there a pair of angels, each carrying a rooster—one of the emblems of Saint Peter.

San Francisco del Átil

Referred to in Jesuit records as Los Siete Príncipes del Átil (The Seven Archangels of Átil), the patronage of this mission was apparently changed to that of Saint Francis of Assisi when the Franciscans arrived in 1768 and made it a *cabecera* with a *visita* at Oquitoa. There is no evidence of a church's having been here in Father Kino's day, although it was reported in 1730 that construction of such a building had been started.[27]

What is known for sure is that the church and missionary's residence at Átil, whose slowly melting adobe ruins can still be seen, were built under the administration of Father Jacobo Sedelmayr of Tubutama when Átil was its *visita*. In March of 1747, Father Sedelmayr reported to the Jesuit Visitor General, "On my return from the sea Gulf of (California) I brought with me from the coast a ranchería of 200 or more gentile Indians [O'odham] who all

Ruins of the 1747 church (left) and the 20th century church at Átil, 1935. George A. Grant

settled down and were baptized in my *pueblo de visita* called Ati. It is 4 leagues downriver from Tubutama. I am building a church there and a house for their administration."[28]

This structure, although now in ruins, has special appeal in that it was the home base from 1756 to 1761 for one of Pimería Alta's more literary Jesuit missionaries, Father Ignaz Pfefferkorn, whose *Sonora: A Description of the Province*

(Tucson: The University of Arizona Press, 1989) is a regional classic.

Father Reyes opined in 1772 that Átil had the potential to become "the most pleasant and prosperous settlement of the Pimería Alta," and in 1788 Father Barbastro reported that the church here, then a *visita* of Tubutama, was one that had been "beautified" by the friars. In 1797, when Father Francisco Yturralde made his official visit, Átil was again a

cabecera, one with two resident missionaries. The Father Visitor said the church and its sacristy formed "two suitable rooms." The walls and floor were of adobe and the roof was made of wooden beams[29]—a scene easily visualized today as one looks at the ruins next to the place of worship presently in use.

San Antonio Paduano del Oquitoa

Oquitoa church, 1996. Nicholas Bleser

Of all the mission churches in the Pimería Alta where religious services continue to be conducted, Oquitoa is the only one that exemplifies perfectly the flat-roofed, hall church characteristic of Jesuit construction in the region.

Indians from this village (whom the Spanish labelled *Soba*) were said to have been responsible for attacking Caborca in 1695 and martyring its Jesuit missionary, Francisco Javier Saeta.[30] In 1723, the village lacked both a church and a house for the missionary. Seven years later, however, a chapel was reported to be under construction. By this time (1730), Oquitoa was a *visita* of Tubutama. Previously it had been under the jurisdiction of the *cabecera* at

Caborca and, later, during the Franciscan period, it would become a *visita* of Átil.[31]

The Franciscan priest who served longest at Oquitoa was Fray Francisco Moyano who arrived from Átil around 1795 and remained until his death in 1818. In 1801, he succeeded Francisco Iturralde as Father President of the missionary priests in the Pimería Alta and it is likely that he transferred the *cabecera* from Átil at that time. Three decades later, in 1830, San Antonio Paduano del Oquitoa was reported to be a *cabecera* without *visitas*.[32]

It is almost certainly this building, whose church and sacristy in 1797 provided "suitable rooms," whose roof was of beams (as it is today), and which was "sheathed on the outside with

brick and lime mortar," that is seen today. A "beautification" project mentioned by Father Barbastro in 1788 and described by Father Yturralde in 1797 probably included the new brick facade with scalloped portal and, inside, the addition of a triumphal arch separating the nave from the sanctuary.[33]

Ruins of the wheat mill at Oquitoa, 1981. Mardith Schuetz–Miller

Monuments in the cemetery at the Oquitoa church, 1984. James Officer

San Diego del Pitiquito

Always a *visita* of Caborca in Jesuit times, a small adobe chapel was under construction here in 1706. By 1730 it was gone, and a second adobe building, one with a straw and dirt roof, was apparently erected in the 1760s after the Pima Rebellion and before the Jesuit

expulsion. This structure was so poorly furnished that when Father Juan Marcelo Díaz, who in 1768 was stationed at the Caborca *cabecera*, went there to say Mass, he had to take all of his equipment with him. In 1772, Father Antonio Reyes wrote of Pitiquito that it had neither a church nor a house for the missionary.[34]

This situation was remedied beginning in the late 1770s when

Father José Matías Moreno started to raise the lime-mortared brick church whose remodelled form one sees at Pitiquito today. Moreno was baptizing Indians at Pitiquito by March of 1776, and he probably started construction then or very soon afterward. It was his successor, Father Pedro Font, who was baptizing people at Pitiquito by January of 1780, who brought the building to its initial state of

Mission San Diego del Pitiquito, 1981. James Officer

completion before his death a little less than two years later. It is ironic that the builders of Pitiquito died in the same year just seven weeks apart: Father Moreno at the hands of Quechan Indians at Yuma on July 17, 1781, and Father Font of natural causes in Pitiquito on September 6, 1781.[35]

Father Yturralde wrote in 1797 that the church and sacristy were "two very fine rooms of brick and lime mortar," there was a vaulted roof, and the floors were of brick.[36]

It appears that many additions and alterations have been made at Pitiquito, both inside and out, since 1781. Records describing these have yet to come to light.

The Handwriting on the Wall

In 1966, a little girl was attending Mass in the church at Pitiquito when her attention began to stray. She looked up at a column on the wall and saw the image of a human skeleton beginning to appear on its surface. The child's mother followed her gaze, and screamed when she, too, saw the apparition. One can imagine the commotion that followed. And as if having a picture of a skeleton materialize were not enough, so did the words MANE THECEL PHARES, a version of the biblical handwriting on the wall recorded in the Book of Daniel (5: 25–28) as MENE, MENE, TEKEL, UPHARSIN, interpreted to mean that King Belshazzar had been found wanting in the scales of justice and that God was about to divide his kingdom and award it to the Medes and Persians.

Later—and calmer—investigation revealed that many paintings decorating the walls of Pitiquito's church had been whitewashed over many years previously. Women had begun to use detergent to clean the white walls, and its chemicals eventually reacted with the lime in the whitewash to disclose the ancient art. Since then, more of these dry frescoes have been uncovered by Mexican conservation experts, and visitors can now enjoy paintings of Lucifer, the Virgin Mary, symbols of the Passion of Christ, attributes of three of the four evangelists, the scales of justice, architectural elements, and other depictions and lettering as yet undeciphered. These works, genuinely folk art, appear to date from the nineteenth century.

Equally interesting are painted frames that probably date from the time the church was finished in its original form about 1781. These are frames around what once were presumably depictions of the fourteen stations of the cross, events in the story of Christ's Passion. These frames for images of the stations, if indeed that is what was being framed, are on the original layer of the walls' surface and were concealed under other coats of plaster and whitewash. Serpents form the vertical sides of one of the frames, and the upper horizontal side is capped with triangles and heads of figures wearing what appear to be ceremonial headdresses. What makes them important is that these modest painted frames may well represent the only place in any church in the Pimería Alta where the hand of an O'odham painter survives.

Bernard L. Fontana

Don Normark, 1987

La Purísima Concepción de Nuestra Señora de Caborca

The first church at Caborca was built soon after October 1694 when Jesuit missionary Francisco Xavier Saeta became its first priest. Father Saeta was martyred in an O'odham uprising in April 1695, and two months later both his house and the church were burned. In 1698 repairs were made on the buildings, and between 1702 and 1706 a replacement church was constructed with the help of carpenters brought to the site by Father Kino. By 1730, however, it had apparently fallen into ruin because Caborca, then a *visita* of Tubutama, was said to be without a proper place of worship.[37]

It appears that sometime between 1743 and 1749 a third church was completed at Caborca, one also destined to be heavily damaged—if not destroyed—in 1751 during the Pima Rebellion when Caborca's resident missionary, Tomás Tello, was killed by the O'odham. When Father Juan Díaz took over for the Franciscans in 1768, he described the Jesuit construction at Caborca as a partially destroyed building of adobe with a roof of straw and dirt. It was nonetheless the *cabecera* with *visitas* at San Diego de Pitiquito and Santa María del Pópulo—earlier San Valentín—de Bísanig.[38]

In 1772 the church at Caborca, according to Father Reyes, had both a sacristy and side chapel as well as a house for the priest. He wrote that in 1771 the missionary at Caborca had wanted to move the site of this Jesuit-built complex to higher ground where it would be less

Mission La Purísima Concepción de Nuestra Señora de Caborca, 1981. James Officer

Main altar, Caborca church, 1894. Wm. Dinwiddie

subject to flooding by the Río Concepción.[39]

Father Barbastro wrote in 1788 that by 1783 the temple at Caborca had been "beautified," suggesting some Franciscan improvements on a Jesuit edifice. In 1792, he observed optimistically that Father José Mora, a man of "little schooling, but very efficient," was following his order to begin a new stone and mortar house of worship at Caborca.[40]

As it turned out, Father Mora left Caborca in 1793. When Father Yturralde made his visit in 1797, the old building with a sacristy with adobe walls and a flat wood-beamed roof was still there, although the floor was tiled.[41]

It was Father Andrés Sánchez who started the present structure no earlier than 1803 if a report written that year by Father Francisco Moyano can be credited. It was finished by May of 1809 under the successive administrations of Fray Santiago Usuastegui and Fray Saturnino Arizeta.[42]

The principal builder at Caborca was Ignacio Gaona, the *maestro albañil* (mason/architect) who had done such a masterful job earlier at Mission San Xavier del Bac. The person who executed the wall paintings inside Caborca's church was probably Gordiano Escalante, a "master painter" resident in the town in 1811.[43]

The Río Concepción cutting into the Caborca church, 1928.
Photographer unknown

Façade of Caborca church, 1992.
James Officer

Given the similarity between the two buildings and the fact that Ignacio Gaona was *maestro albañil* for both, there can be no question that the Caborca church was modelled after that of the earlier San Xavier del Bac. The somewhat less graceful, squattier appearance of La Purísima Concepción de Nuestra Señora de Caborca is occasioned by the fact that its

facade is four feet wider and two feet shorter than that at San Xavier even as its twin towers are eleven feet shorter than San Xavier's completed west tower. The interior of San Xavier (136 feet 6 inches long from portal to sanctuary rear by 21 feet 7 inches wide; 2,946 square feet) is larger than that at Caborca (129 feet 8 inches by 19 feet 2 inches; 2,486 square feet). These square footages are exclusive of transepts, sacristies, and spaces in the bell towers.[44]

General deterioration and damage from floods began to eat away at the rear of the church and its northerly convento wing beginning in 1890 when a room collapsed. A large room fell in 1899, and in 1915 the back of the convento and two more rooms closer to the main altar were ravaged. The sanctuary with its main altar was taken out in 1917. Restoration began in 1957 to mark the one-hundredth anniversary of the defeat of the Crabb filibustering expedition, but in January 1993 a flooding Río Concepción destroyed the rebuilt convento and most of the rebuilt north sacristy.[45] Unless drastic measures are taken to re-channel the adjacent river, such destructive flooding is sure to plague this magnificent structure's uncertain future.

Santa María del Pópulo de Bísanig

About ten miles west of Caborca on the north side of the Río Concepción lie the fairly imposing adobe ruins of a church built by the Jesuits sometime between 1730, when there was none there, and 1768, when the Franciscans took over at the *cabecera* of Caborca. Always a *visita* of Caborca, this O'odham community had been called San Valentín de Bísanig by Father Kino and he had seen to the construction of its first house of worship in 1706, one that apparently disappeared during the ensuing twenty-four years.[46]

Caborca's first Franciscan minister found an adobe church here with a dirt-covered roof, but one without furnishings. Father Reyes, who called Bísanig "San Juan," said in 1772 that the place had both a church and house for the missionary. He also said the O'odham who lived here preferred to fish along the shores of the Gulf of California as their principal means of subsistence, a means of livelihood not ordinarily associated with desert dwelling Pimans.[47]

Surviving Franciscan records indicate that friars routinely baptized Papagos and captive Indians (*Nijoras*) being raised among Papagos at Bísanig between 1774 and 1797. Besides there having been a beamed, flat-roofed adobe church and sacristy here in 1797, Father Yturralde observed the floors were of *argamasa*, lime mortar with a fine finish, one often with powdered fired bricks having been

Ruins of Mission Santa María del Pópulo de Bísanig, 1987.
Edwin Smart

added to the mix to provide a red colored surface.[48]

Even as Caborca was undergoing construction between 1803 and 1809, the Jesuit-built edifice at this *visita* was being renovated. It remained as an outlier of Caborca at least until 1830. Although the site has never been reoccupied, the seldom-visited ruins, standing in a broad plain, are now in use as a cemetery.[49]

Nuestra Señora del Pilar y Santiago de Cocóspera

Situated on a high bluff overlooking the Río Babasac, an eastern tributary of the Río Magdalena, are what surely are the most imposing church ruins in Sonora. In the 1980s it became necessary for Mexico's Instituto Nacional de Antropología e Historia—the caretaker of many of that country's historic structures—to erect an unsightly scaffolding at the front of the building to prevent the Franciscan-added brick facade from pulling away from the original Jesuit adobe wall and collapsing into a pile of rubble. Even this distraction, however, cannot conceal the former magnificence of what was once the most unusual construction in the Pimería Alta.

Cocóspera was probably visited by Father Kino soon after

Cocóspera Valley and the distant Sierra Azul (right) viewed from the site of Mission Cocóspera, 1935. George Grant

1687, although the earliest mention of it in his memoirs concerns a visit made there early in 1689 by Father Visitor Manuel Gonzáles. Either later in 1689 or in 1690, Father Juan del Castillejo became the mission's first resident priest, but he served less than a year. From the outset, Nuestra Señora del Pilar y Santiago, famed in Spanish legend, had been made patrons of the village.[50]

In 1697 Kino reported that Cocóspera had the "good beginnings of a church and house," beginnings apparently brought to completion by February, 1698 when "the village, the church, and the father's residence were sacked and burned" by an attacking force of some three hundred Jocomes, Sumas, and Apaches. Cocóspera's position at the eastern edge of the Pimería Alta left it exposed throughout its active history to almost unimpeded raiding and revenge warfare by Apaches living in the mountains and valleys to the northeast and east.[51]

Never one to be deterred, the always-optimistic Father Kino gave orders in 1700 "to roof the little church," and in 1701 he saw to the erection of *torreones* (towers) as an aid in defending the settlement. The following year he began to erect an adobe church on a far grander scale. Cocóspera and Remedios were then *visitas* of his *cabecera* at Dolores, and he carried out a building program in these places at the same time. Kino was proud of this work, and he observed that as good as his church at Dolores was, those at Remedios and Cocóspera "turned out even better, for they have transepts, etc." His account of their construction is a detailed one:

In these months and the following I ordered the necessary wood cut for the pine framework, sills, flooring, etc. I went to the interior and brought more than seven hundred dollars' worth of clothing, tools and heavy ware and from other places I obtained more than three thousand dollars' worth, which shortly and with ease were paid for with goods, provisions, and cattle of the three rich districts. I

76

invited some (Indians) from the frontier for the work on these buildings, and there came far and away more than I had asked for; and very especially, for entire months, the many inhabitants of the great new pueblo of San Francisco Xavier del Bac, which is sixty leagues distant to the north, worked and built on the three pueblos of this place and of my administration. In this way many adobes were made in the two pueblos of Nuestra Señora de los Remedios and Nuestra Señora del Pilar y Santiago de Cocóspera; and high and strong walls were made for two large and good churches, with their two spacious chapels, which form transepts, with good and pleasing arches. The timbers were brought from the neighboring mountains and pineries, and the two good buildings were roofed, and provided with cupolas, small lanterns, etc. I managed almost all the year to go nearly every week through the three pueblos, looking after both spiritual and temporal things, and the rebuilding of the two above-mentioned new churches.[52]

The new temple was dedicated in January 1704 "with all the ceremonies and benedictions which our Holy Mother Church commands, according to the holy Roman ritual." Present among the invited guests was the "captain of the Yumas, with many of his people," who had come all the way from the lower Colorado River bringing with them as gifts shells of the blue abalone, a

marine animal absent in the Gulf of California but present along the Pacific coast of California. Kino correctly surmised that trade in such shells proved that California was connected to the Pimería Alta by land and was not an island.[53]

After Kino's death in 1711, Cocóspera fell into decline. In 1720 it was reported that the physical plant was in bad repair. By 1730 the church was

essentially in ruins, and in 1746 Apaches delivered the *coup de grâce* by torching its remaining timbers and other wooden elements. Despite its ruined condition, Cocóspera took in O'odham refuges from Dolores and Remedios when those places were abandoned in the 1740s.[54]

In 1751, the Father Visitor of the Pimería Alta went to Cocóspera, which was then a *visita* of Santa María de Soamca (today's Santa Cruz, Sonora). Here he

"preached twice to the Indians" who, he said, "did not know how to pray and had no catechist." Moreover, he complained that the church linens were dirty and wrote to the minister at the *cabecera* saying he should have the linens taken to Soamca to be washed—as if the minister, whose people daily feared for their lives in the face of Apache raids, had nothing more important to worry about.[55]

Engraving based on John Ross Browne drawing of Mission Cocóspera, 1864.

No sooner had the first Franciscan arrived at his *cabecera* of Santa María de Soamca in 1768 when Apaches attacked. He and the Soamca O'odham relocated to the Cocóspera *visita*, and in 1772 Father Reyes wrote that this Franciscan and "his Indians" were building a "new" church, although they were probably effecting major repairs on the Jesuit-built adobe structure, some of whose walls could well have been those of the edifice dedicated by Father Kino and others in 1704. Either way, their efforts were halted when in 1776 Apaches attacked once more and burned whatever they could.[56]

The savior of Cocóspera,

Ruins of Mission Nuestra Señora del Pilar y Santiago de Cocóspera before stabilization efforts, 1981.
James Officer

Father Juan de Santiesteban, arrived here in 1784 and remained for seventeen years. Inspection of today's ruins reveals that Father Santiesteban sandwiched the sun-dried adobe walls of an earlier Jesuit church, possibly that dedicated by Father Kino in 1704 and which had undergone many subsequent repairs and alterations. Besides new exterior and interior

surfaces for the old walls, using a combination of sun-dried adobes and fired brick and lime mortar the friar added a new facade as well as a baptistery, sacristy, choir loft, and twin bell towers, each with a spiral staircase of mesquite wood. The roof of the building

was unique among Pimería Alta temples. The exterior surface was a pitched roof covered with fired clay tiles—the first of record in the upper Pimería—set in lime mortar. The interior ceiling above the choir loft and nave was in the shape of a plastered barrel vault formed by dressed beams laid at right angles across the top of three arches. Small transverse poles, possibly ocotillo stems, were used to fill the spaces between the beams and to hold the plaster vault. The roof above the sanc-

tuary, which remained until as recently as 1935, was a burned brick barrel vault.[57]

Father Santiesteban left Cocóspera in 1801, and other Franciscans were assigned there until 1836. With the departure of the last Franciscan, and with Apache raiding on the increase, the population of Cocóspera rapidly declined.[58]

In 1851, United States Boundary Commissioner John Russell Bartlett, who visited the site, said it had been abandoned "about six years before" because of Apache inroads. He found the church along with its towers and dome in a good state of preservation. Its interior, he wrote

. . . must have been very beautiful in its time, when its numerous niches were filled with statues, and its walls covered with paintings. The gilded and painted ornaments upon the walls and ceiling still remained, consisting of crucifixes, doves, and other sacred emblems, surrounded by inscriptions, scrolls, and flowers, which displayed more taste than we had before seen in such buildings. Several wooden figures still stood about the altar; but the pictures were all gone. Bats were already in full possession of the edifice, and hung from the projecting walls and corners, like so many black ornaments; while the swallows which were flitting about us had also taken up their abode here, and added their mud-built nests to its interior decorations.[59]

Cocóspera was temporarily occupied by would-be French colonists in 1851 and 1852,[60] but those short-lived efforts gave way to intermittent abandonment alternating with times when squatters camped there. United States Treasury agent and journalist John Ross Browne paid the ruined church a visit in 1864. He wrote

. . . A more desolate-looking place than Cocospera does not perhaps exist in Sonora. A few Mexican and Indian huts, huddled around a ruinous old church, with a ghostly population of

Greasers, Yaqui Indians, skeleton dogs, and seedy sheep, is all that attracts the eye of a stranger under the best of circumstances. . . . At the date of our visit the Apaches had just cleaned out the community of nearly all the cattle and sheep it possessed, killed one man, and filled the souls of the remainder with fear and tribulation, so that the place presented a very depressed appearance.[61]

After he retired from the Mexican army in 1851, Colonel José María Elías González took up residence in the Cocóspera Valley.

In spite of Apaches, he was able to operate his ranch in the valley until his death in 1864 at the age of seventy-two. Other members of his family continued to reside here, and in the late 1950s some of them erected the small burial chapel next to the Cocóspera ruins. The first whose remains were placed in a crypt here was José Elías Suárez, a nephew several times removed of the colonel. José Elías Suárez was a brother of Francisco Elías Suárez, governor of Sonora from 1927 to 1931.[62]

San José de Ímuris

Although visited briefly by Franciscans in an abortive effort in 1645 to extend their mission field toward the west, the O'odham at Ímuris were left largely to their own devices until the arrival of Father Kino in 1687. Kino visited Ímuris as early as March 1687, but it was the 1690s before some kind of chapel was built here. Throughout virtually all of its life as a mission, Ímuris was a *visita* of San Ignacio, and only rarely did it have a resident priest.

It is unclear how many chapels may have been built at

Ímuris in the seventeenth and eighteenth centuries. Father Reyes wrote in his 1772 report that the church and house were nearly in ruins, and by 1797 there was not enough there to warrant an inspection by Father Visitor Yturralde whose narrative of his visitation makes no mention of the place.[63]

When the village—whose O'odham population had been displaced by Mexicans by 1801— was visited by United States Boundary Commissioner J. R. Bartlett in 1851, he found an "an improvement . . . in the adobe houses here; they were all capped with brick or tile," perhaps a tribute to Father Santiesteban's earlier innovation at nearby

Nuestro Señor de Esquipulas, the Cristo Negro (Black Christ) of San José de Ímuris, 1978. John Schaefer

Cocóspera. Bartlett also said the church "appeared quite new," no doubt a post-Franciscan construction.[64]

Today's church at Ímuris is a twentieth-century building from foundation to ceiling. What gave it special historical interest, however, is that it shelters a large crucifix bearing the figure of what until 1995 was a *Cristo Negro* (Black Christ), Nuestro Señor de Esquipulas.

The cult of Nuestro Señor de Esquipulas has its origins in sixteenth-century Guatemala. In one version of its history, the Mayan Indians, having seen the cruelty of the white man and having therefore become suspicious of a white Christ, commissioned a woodcarver to sculpture a Christ out of balsam and orange wood whose natural color resembled that of their skin. The figure was mounted on a cross, and in time, smoke from burning votive candles and incense turned him black. In 1595 the crucifix was taken

Mission San José de Ímuris, 1996.
Nicholas Bleser

to the southeastern Guatemalan town of Esquipulas where it was set up in a little chapel near several health-giving springs. The image soon became famous for its miraculous cures, and according to oral tradition, one of those thus cured in 1737 was the archbishop of Guatemala. He was so grateful that he had a large sanctuary—now a basilica—erected to house the figure, a church completed in 1758. The fame of the Black Christ

spread far and wide throughout Latin America and similar images began to be made and established in different communities, almost always in association with healing waters.[65]

According to an official report submitted in 1843, one of the rooms in the convento of the *visita* of San Agustín del Tucson contained statues of saints, including "a majestic representation of the miraculous image of Our Lord of Esquipulas." In 1856, presumably when the Mexican troops left Tucson, it was taken to Ímuris where it can still be seen in the church, although in 1995 its black finish was removed and Our Lord of Esquipulas became a generalized image of the crucified Christ.[66]

In Sonora, there is still a Black Christ in the old mission church at Aconchi on the Río Sonora, and in New Mexico, the crucifix of Esquipulas is in the sanctuary at Chimayó—both carved images dating from the first half of the nineteenth century.

San Ignacio de Cabórica

Father Kino was at San Ignacio in 1687 the day after he had first

arrived at Dolores. He described Cabórica as a "very good post . . . inhabited by affable people"—as it continues to be. It was three years before a missionary was stationed here and three more years before

anyone was permanently assigned. Whatever church may have existed before 1693 when Father Agustín de Campos began his incredible forty-two-year tenure at San Ignacio is likely to have been no more than a ramada. It is not even clear a religious structure was in existence in 1695 when the O'odham rebelled throughout the Pimería Alta. Kino mentions that Father Campos escaped with his soldier escort, and that houses, storerooms, and three sets of vestments were burned, but says nothing about a church.[67]

There was still no proper house of worship 1699, but in August of 1702, Father Campos buried San Xavier del Bac's first minister, Francisco Gonzalvo, on the gospel side in front of the altar of San Ignacio's church. The building was described in 1730 as being "deteriorated," and seven years later, Father Campos, in ill health and, in the minds of many of his fellow Jesuits, in failing mental condition, was removed from his post in spite of O'odham protests at losing their minister. He died in July 1737 at Baserac on the Río Bavispe en route to the Jesuit college at Chihuahua, a broken and broken-hearted sixty-eight-year-old man.[68]

Father Campos's replacement at San Ignacio was Father Gaspar Stiger. He remained here until his death in 1762 and was succeeded by Francisco Pauer who was in charge at San Ignacio until the Jesuits' expulsion in 1767.[69]

When the Franciscans took over in 1768, San Ignacio was

Mission San Ignacio de Cabórica, 1992. James Officer

Interior of the San Ignacio church, 1968. James Griffith

Main entrance, Mission San Ignacio, 1894. Wm. Dinwiddie

made the *cabecera* while Santa María Magdalena and Ímuris were its *visitas*. Father Reyes, writing in 1772, said the church at Cabórica was "adorned in the inside with three small side chapels," and the missionary's house, which had been partially destroyed in 1770, was next to it.[70]

Father Francisco Sánchez Zúñiga arrived at San Ignacio in 1772 and either made major alterations on the old structure or built an entirely new one—more

likely the former—before his departure in 1780. This lovely barrel vaulted and domed edifice, one which features a mesquite spiral staircase leading to the roof in its west tower, is that which visitors to San Ignacio see today. Given that most of the walls are of sun-dried adobe veneered on the exterior with fired bricks, the physical evidence makes it appear most probable that Father Sánchez Zúñiga did for San Ignacio what Father Santiesteban did later for Cocóspera: make a Franciscan church out of a Jesuit one. Certainly the facade, barrel vault, dome, and towers, all of burned brick and lime mortar, can be attributed to Father Sánchez. Whether the adobe church so extensively remodelled between 1772 and 1780 was that built by Father Campos and consistently maintained, with alternations, by his Jesuit successors or is a later Jesuit construction is presently impossible to say.[71]

The O'odham population of San Ignacio began to dwindle toward the end of the eighteenth century. By 1818 it was reported that for every one Indian, the missionary ministered to three dozen *Españoles y Castas*.[72] Like nearly all the other former mission communities in the Pimería Alta, it is today wholly a non-Indian town.

Mesquite spiral stairway in bell tower of the San Ignacio church, ca. 1940. Edward Ronstadt

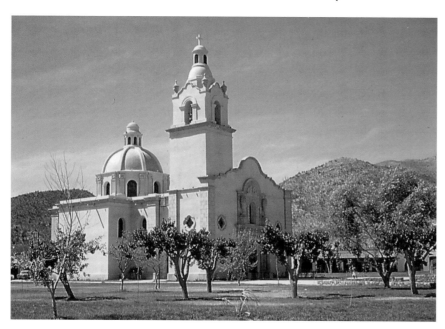

Mission Santa María Magdalena, 1971. James Officer

Santa María Magdalena

Even though now famous because it became the burial place of Father Eusebio Kino, Santa María Magdalena was also a *visita* throughout the Jesuit period. The church and house there were being built in 1705 under the administration of Father Agustín de Campos of San Ignacio. In 1706, Father Kino personally lent a hand with construction.[73]

Father Kino had just finished building a new chapel in Magdalena, one dedicated to San Fran-

Mission Santa María Magdalena, 1832: *left*, Perez Llera church (1852); *center*, Campos church **(1705–06); *right*, St. Francis Xavier chapel (1711).** Drawn by Jorge Olvera

cisco Xavier, when he died there in 1711. In 1730, the temple built by Father Campos with Kino's help and which included an imposing bell tower on its own slab foundation, was described as being deteriorated. Father Reyes wrote in 1772 that the house for the missionary was "entirely in ruins," and the church was "large but dilapidated and only a chapel to San Francisco Xavier has any decent furnishings."[74]

If Father Reyes was right about the priest's house, the situation was corrected before November of 1776 when Father Pedro Font, recently returned from his overland expedition to Alta California, was stationed here. Apaches, Seris, and apostate O'odham attacked Magdalena that month and Font described the assault in great detail. From it we learn that his flat-roofed adobe house, which may or may not have been attached to the church, was hall shaped, consisting of "seven rooms in a row, one after the other. There was a kitchen, then a storeroom followed by two other rooms, and then another larger one which was a parlor; finally, there were two medium-sized rooms. The whole was of adobe with a roof of grass and earth." Before being frightened away by reinforcements coming from nearby San Ignacio, the attackers were able to torch the roof over five of the seven rooms. They also broke into the church, carried off the vestments, spilled the holy oils, ripped the linens from statues. They took from its case "a lovely image of San Francisco Xavier," which they threw on the floor, breaking its arm. For good measure, they ruined the baptismal font and candlesticks.[75]

That Franciscans effected

repairs on the Campos/Kino building is clear from the 1797 report of Father Yturralde's visitation. "I inspected the church," he wrote, "which is a single pretty and respectable room whose construction is of adobe with a wooden roof that has been covered with lime mortar. The sacristy still is not completed."[76]

All traces of the 1705–06 structure have since disappeared, although its ruins and the church now in use can be seen in depictions rendered in 1851, 1864, and 1879 respectively by John Russell Bartlett, John Ross Browne, and Alphonse Pinart.[77] While the chapel in which Father Kino is buried has also disappeared, part of its stone footings can now be viewed adjacent to his skeletal remains under roof and glass in the Kino Memorial Plaza. The church on this central plaza today is the latest Franciscan structure in the Pimería Alta, a building erected between 1830 and 1832 by Father José Pérez Llera. It was heavily remodeled in the late 1950s essentially in its present form.[78]

Church at Santa Ana Viejo, 1920.
Frank Pinkley

Santa Ana Viejo

Never a mission, the viceregal-period community of Santa Ana, today's Santa Ana Viejo which lies on the west side of the Río Magdalena opposite the modern town of Santa Ana, boasts an interesting church, one possibly built early in the nineteenth century with later additions. Santa Ana began its life at least as early as 1739 as a Spanish ranch, among the earliest non-Indian ranches in the Pimería Alta. In 1772 Father Reyes observed that the place, "a ranch, or breeding farm, for cattle and horses," was "popularly called the Real de Santa Ana." He said it had neither church nor a minister of the Doctrine, a situation seemingly unchanged in 1775 when Juan Bautista de Anza's overland colonizing expedition passed through here en route to Alta California.[79]

The church now to be seen in Santa Ana Viejo underwent a major alteration completed in 1894 and another in 1992. In Sonora, churches tend to be symbols of community, and the church's excellent condition is indicative of the pride people living there take in themselves.

Los Santos Ángeles de Guevavi

Now one of three units of Arizona's Tumacacori National Historical Park, the adobe ruins of Los Santos Ángeles de Guevavi lie on the east bank of the Santa Cruz River south of Tumacacori about ten miles north of the International Boundary. They are the product, ultimately, of an initial brief visit paid here in January, 1691, by—who else?—Father Eusebio Francisco Kino. Father Kino christened the O'odham village San Gabriel after one of the archangels. In 1732, a Jesuit successor added San Rafael as a patron, and in 1744 still another missionary decided on San Miguel as the name. Thus was Guevavi under the watchful care of three archangels, Los Santos Ángeles, although by 1774 they had already begun to look the other way when Apaches forced its abandonment.[80]

In 1701, Guevavi was made the *cabecera* with *visitas* at the nearby O'odham villages of San Cayetano de Tumacácori, San Luis del Bacoancos, and Los Santos Reyes de Sonoita. Its first minister arrived, and Father Kino wrote

that "in a few months were finished a house and a church, small but neat, and we laid the foundations of a church and a large house." It was Kino who had ordered that "the neat little church" be roofed and whitewashed.[81]

The first resident Jesuit left Guevavi before the end of 1701 and it was thirty-one years before anyone else was assigned to the community. By 1722, when Father Campos of San Ignacio visited Guevavi, the house, small church, and unfinished larger church and house apparently had disappeared.[82]

The Jesuit enterprise in Pimería Alta was bolstered in 1732 with the arrival of three new missionaries, one of whom, Johann Baptist Grazhoffer, was assigned to Guevavi. The elder Juan Bautista de Anza had seen to the construction at Guevavi of a little house to accommodate the new minister, and Grazhoffer was able to conduct services beneath a sturdy, well-roofed ramada.[83]

Father Grazhoffer died at Guevavi a year after his arrival, and his immediate successor was there a little more than a year before he was assigned elsewhere. After 1737, matters improved and Guevavi was steadily manned by Jesuits until the Pima Rebellion of

Archaeology in progress at Mission Guevavi, 1965.
Bernard Fontana

1751 and, subsequently, until their expulsion in 1767.

Guevavi seems to have gone for years without a proper church. Finally, however, in the summer of 1751 a master builder, Don Joachín de Cásares of Arizpe, arrived on site. Father Joseph Garrucho, Guevavi's minister, had decided on a major building project. Historian John Kessell tells what happened:

. . . Plans called for, or at least came to include, a rectangular church whose inside dimensions were not particularly impressive, about fifteen by fifty feet. The new structure was to be built on the extreme east edge of the mesilla with its long axis lying roughly north-south and its main doors facing south onto the village plaza. Tabular slabs of local conglomerate rock cemented with mud mortar, Don Joachín and Father Joseph agreed, would provide a solid foundation. The walls of sun-dried adobes set in mud mortar were to be all of three feet thick, plastered with mud, white-washed, and finally decorated inside with various colors. The flat roof would rest on *vigas*, large beams spanning the building's short axis. A door through the west wall of the church was to lead out onto a patio enclosed on the other three sides by rooms one deep with their doors opening onto the patio. In this *convento*, measuring overall some 90 by 105 feet, Father Joseph would have his quarters, perhaps a small personal chapel, the Indian school, a kitchen, refectory, and whatever storage and work rooms space permitted. Here at Guevavi Joseph Garrucho would leave, if nothing else, a house of God where none comparable had previously stood.

Presumably master-builder Cásares brought with him to Guevavi artisans and assistants. For unskilled labor, he depended of course on the mission's neophytes. They would supply the muscle, albeit at their own less-than-frantic pace. Commenting on native building crews, Father Sedelmayr once wrote (in 1754): "Their manner of working was to gather between eight and nine and to quit about four. The ones who dug the earth did so seated. Those who carried two small balls of mud did so, then sat down to rest. The others also worked at this pace. But because there were many of them, something was accomplished."[84]

A good deal is known about the particulars of the construction of Guevavi, not through documentary records, but thanks to physical examination of the ruins and to archaeology carried out here over the years.[85]

Whatever damage was done to the new church and living quarters at Guevavi during the 1751 Pima Rebellion—and both were spared the torch—was apparently patched and renovated after 1754 by the mission's new minister.[86]

When the Franciscans took over the *cabecera* of Guevavi in 1768, its *visitas* were San Ignacio de Sonoitac, San José de Tumacácori, and San Cayetano de Calabazas. Father Reyes's 1772 report said that Guevavi's temple was adorned with two altars and a small side chapel with paintings in gilded frames, and its sacristy had everything needed for the altar and divine services.[87]

By 1772, however, the end for this adobe-walled outpost had been assured by Apache hostility. Father Reyes's report incorrectly listed Guevavi as the *cabecera*, because in 1770 or 1771 it had been transferred to Tumacácori. A report written at Tumacácori in 1773 said only nine families continued to live at Guevavi, while a year later, Tumacácori's only *visita* was that at Calabazas. Los Santos Ángeles de Guevavi was abandoned, with only roofless adobe walls and written words as a reminder to posterity.[88]

San José de Tumacácori

When he first visited the O'odham village of Tumacácori in 1691, which was probably on the east side of the Santa Cruz River oppo-site today's Tumacacori, Father Kino blessed it with the name of San Cayetano. By 1697, the Indians had built an "adobe and flat-roofed house" in anticipation of a resident missionary. In the meantime, it was used by itinerant missionaries and other Spaniards.[87]

Whatever Jesuit activity occurred at Tumacácori between Kino's death and the 1751 rebellion seems to have been minimal, with reference to it in the historical record being sporadic at best. Father Visitor Jacobo Sedelmayr neglected even to mention the place during his 1751 visitation of Pimería Alta missions.

After the Pima Rebellion of 1751, San Cayetano de Tumacácori was moved from the east to the west side of the Santa Cruz River and given a new patronage, that of San José. Early in 1753, the Jesuits dedicated the new location, with its new saint's name, with proper ceremony. By 1757, they had built a new hall-shaped adobe church measuring some sixty feet by twenty feet, the stabilized outlines of which can still be seen on the grounds of the Tumacácori unit of Tumacacori National Historical Park.[90]

Franciscans began to erect a new house of worship at Tumacácori in 1802, five years after completion of San Xavier del Bac and a year before work began at Caborca. The Jesuit-constructed adobe building was described as being too narrow as well as in an advanced stage of deterioration. Work was behind schedule in January of 1807 because of foul weather.[91] But it was not only the elements that delayed matters. There was a lack of skilled artisans and, more than anything else, Tumacácori was short of money. The sale of four thousand head of mission cattle to a rancher in 1821 promised a solution, but efforts on the church were halted once again in 1822 when the rancher failed to

Church at Mission San José de Tumacácori, 1994. George H. H. Huey

Nave of church at Mission San José de Tumacácori, 1994. George H. H. Huey

Church and *convento*, Mission San José de Tumacácori, 1890s. D. R. Paynes

Bell in church tower, Mission San José de Tumacácori, 1994.
George H. H. Huey

pay installments on his purchase.[92]

It had been Fray Narciso Gutiérrez, a minister at Tumacácori since 1794, who in 1802 had the church laid out in cruciform plan and had intended that the roof would be brick, vaulted and domed. His model was Mission San Xavier del Bac. However, it was left to Father Gutiérrez's successor in 1820, Fray Juan Bautista Estelric, aided by his master builder, Félix Antonio Bustamente of Sombrerete, Zacatecas, to simplify the plan by eliminating the vaulted transepts. What had been intended to be

cruciform became rectangular instead. Fray Ramón Liberós, who completed the job about 1828, had been forced finally to compromise even further by substituting a wood-and-mud flat roof for a vaulted brick one over the nave, the only dome surviving in the original plan being built over the sanctuary, and the only vault over the adjoining sacristy. Moreover, sun-dried adobes outnumbered fired bricks in the structure's walls, making it far less permanent than San Xavier's brick/stone/lime mortar building.[93]

Ruins of the mission at Calabazas, 1929. George Grant

San Cayetano de Calabazas

No mention is made of Calabazas in the historical record until November of 1756 when Father Francisco Pauer, the Jesuit minister at Guevavi, relocated seventy-eight O'odham neophytes from their village of Toacuquita to this new location. It lies between Guevavi and Tumacácori on a bluff on the east side of the Santa Cruz River just upstream from its junction with Sonoita Creek.[94]

Since San Cayetano de Tumacácori was by then San José

de Tumacácori, there was good reason Las Calabazas should be awarded the patronage of Saint Cajetan (San Cayetano), the 1524 co-founder of the Theatine Clerks Regular, a strict religious order whose members modelled their lives on those of the Apostles. Cayetano—whose carved wooden likeness, which may once have been at Calabazas, can now be seen in the museum in the visitors' center at the Tumacácori unit of Tumacacori National Historical Park—was canonized in 1671, just twenty years before Father Kino bestowed his name originally on Tumacácori.

Calabazas possessed neither church nor cemetery in January of 1760, but by May of 1761 the minister of its *cabecera* at Guevavi wrote of Calabazas that it had "a new house with door and lock. The church I leave (to my successor) nearly half built," suggesting it was still roofless. The edifice had to await the arrival of Franciscans who managed to complete the flat-roofed adobe building in 1772 or 1773, just about the time they moved their headquarters from Guevavi to Tumacácori.[95]

It wasn't long before the new church was christened in battle. A group of Apaches, apostate O'odham, and Seris—possibly some of the same men who had attacked Magdalena and other Pimería Alta communities the previous year—swooped down on Calabazas in 1777. "They sacked and set fire to it, burning all the houses, the church, and the granary with more than a hundred *fanegas* of maize. The mission Indians put up a stiff defense killing thirteen of the enemy at a cost of seven of ours gravely wounded with little hope of survival."[96]

Gente de razón (people of reason)—non-Indians and Christian Indians not living in mission communities—moved into the Santa Cruz valley in growing numbers in the early decades of the nineteenth century. By 1808, several such families had moved into Calabazas, and this in spite of the fact that in 1807 the title to Calabazas lands had been awarded to the Tumacácori O'odham.

The settlers must have fixed up the Calabazas chapel given the fact that in 1818 it provided the location for a wedding. However, permanent tranquility was not to be. Apaches attacked the place in 1830 and "set fire to its buildings and chapel, carrying off all the sacred vessels and vestments from the latter." While cowboys from Tumacácori continued to run cattle in the vicinity, the 1830 attack discouraged anyone from living there for more than the next two decades.[97]

In 1844 Calabazas was sold at auction to the brother-in-law of sometimes Sonoran governor Manuel María Gándara. In 1852, Gándara struck a deal with three Germans and a Frenchman to operate the Calabazas ranch. The Frenchman and one of the Germans moved in, and by April of 1853 they seem to have repaired the old adobe church and converted it into their living quarters. They also added a long rectangular dormitory on the north to house workers and their families.[98]

Calabazas, like the lands of Guevavi and Tumacácori, became part of the United States with ratification of the Gadsden Purchase in June 1854. Mexican soldiers, who had remained in Tucson to protect the citizens from Apaches, withdrew from the Gadsden Purchase territory early in 1856 and the Gándara ranch came to an end. The ranch house which was the old Jesuit church, however, was due for re-use. Late in 1856 it became the temporary home of Major Enoch Steen, commander of four companies of the First Regiment of United States Dragoons who established Camp Moore at Calabazas as the first military post in the New Mexico Territory's Gadsden Purchase area (which in 1863 became the southern portion of the newly created Arizona Territory). Steen moved Camp Moore to Sonoita Creek in 1857, but his house, the former chapel, was taken over by the United States Deputy Collector of the Revenue for New Mexico whose job it was to collect duty on goods coming into the United States from adjacent Mexico.[99]

Following the departure of the Collector of the Revenue from Calabazas, it is possible, although by no means certain, the adobe was used as a temporary dwelling for at least four or five more families and once may have housed the local post office. What does seem certain, though, is that by 1878 the old church of San Cayetano de Calabazas had given up the ghost with nothing remaining except its roofless shell, a small part of which is now protected as the Calabazas unit of Tumacácori National Historical Park.

Mission San Xavier del Bac, 1894.
Wm. Dinwiddie

Facing page: **church at Mission San Xavier del Bac, ca. 1972.** Helga Teiwes

San Xavier del Bac

The great house of worship presently at San Xavier del Bac, whose interior is the decorative *pièce de résistance* of Pimería Alta churches as well as of all Spanish-period churches within the continental boundaries of today's United States, is the second in this O'odham village. Father Kino, whose first visit to the O'odham community of Wa:k (Bac) was in 1692, began to build a church here in 1700. It apparently never got beyond its foundations, however, and in 1751 the Jesuit Father Visitor Jacobo Sedelmayr said of the Indian community, "It is still very backward without a catechist, without obedience, and without any church other than a ramada and a wretched house. It is clear to see that this village has been visited very little."[100]

San Xavier's first church, other than a ramada, was a flat-roofed, hall-shaped adobe building begun shortly after the arrival of Jesuit missionary Father Alonso Espinosa in 1756. It was serviceable at least by 1763, although given the fact that Espinosa failed to level the site and there were no stone foundations, there must have been structural problems from the outset.

Father Reyes's 1772 report said of Father Espinosa's church that it was "of medium capacity, adorned with two side chapels with paintings in gilded frames." It also had a sacristy, apparently behind the sanctuary and main altar. The building was somewhat unusual in that the *vigas*, instead of spanning its entire width from wall to wall, ran from outer walls to the tops of longitudinal beams supported on a row of wooden columns standing along the length of the church. Persons entering

Bas–relief angels on a pilaster on the main altarpiece of the San Xavier church. Paul Schwartzbaum

the main portal on the south were immediately confronted by a row of posts down the middle of the nave to the sanctuary.[101]

The adobe church built by Father Espinosa was the one inherited by Father Francisco Garcés when he arrived at San Xavier in 1768 as its first Franciscan minister. The peripatetic friar seems always to have been more interested in people than in buildings, in seeking new souls than in properly enclosing spaces for religious worship—although it was he who built an elaborate fortified residence complex with *torreones* in his *visita* of San Agustín del Tucson by February 1771. By 1772, the year of Father Reyes's report, an adobe chapel with a roof of beams was under construction there.[102]

Improvements in the architectural situation at San Xavier had to await the arrival in 1776 of Father Juan Bautista Velderrain, a Basque friar who in 1774 and 1775 had overseen construction of a fired brick church at the Lower Pima (Southern O'odham) village of San Ignacio de Suaqui Grande.[103]

Although 1783 is a date commonly given for the beginning of the present magnificent edifice at San Xavier, 1781 or soon after is far more likely. Velderrain was a builder with a proven track record.

He arrived at San Xavier when Franciscans were about to launch a campaign of new church construction in the Pimería Alta. And most significantly of all, the former president of the Pimería Alta missions, Father Barbastro, writing in mid-1788 ostensibly about the period 1768–1783, included San Xavier among new brick churches with vaulted roofs that by then—either 1783 or 1788—had replaced earlier (Jesuit) structures.[104]

Building San Xavier was an expensive proposition, but Father Velderrain was able to borrow $7,000 pesos—the equivalent of more than twenty years of a missionary's salary—from a businessman, Don Antonio Herreros. The friar's only collateral was wheat from crops not yet even planted—almost as if he expected Don Antonio to join him in his vows of poverty. The good Basque was never able to repay the debt; "spitting blood," he died at San Xavier in 1790, the new church still undecorated and otherwise unfinished.[105]

It was Father Velderrain's successor at San Xavier, Father Juan Bautista Llorens, who oversaw completion by 1797. In 1804, the Spanish commandant of the Tucson *presidio* offered the "conservative estimate" that by then the building expense was

$40,000 pesos. Because of the threat from Apaches, the salaries of the artisans, enticed to the frontier from somewhere farther south in Mexico, had to be doubled. "The reason for the ornate church at this last outpost of the frontier," he wrote, "is not only to congregate Christian Pimas of the San Xavier village, but also to attract by its sheer beauty the unconverted Papagos and Gila Pimas beyond the frontier."[106]

Sometime early in the nineteenth century, probably in the 1820s, Father Espinosa's old church was torn down and its adobes, wooden columns, and ceiling beams were re-used to build a convento wing—still here today—extending east from the east bell tower of the Franciscan structure. Today's church itself has interior and exterior walls of fired bricks set in lime mortar with an interior core filled with stone rubble over which lime mortar was poured periodically as the walls went up.[106]

The east bell tower, as well as interior decoration of a room apparently intended for large meetings of friars, was never finished, a result of a growing debt and a lack of funds or goods with which to repay it. Although the names of the decorators of San Xavier's interior remain unknown, Ignacio Gaona, who in 1801 at age

Nave, crossing, and sanctuary, Mission San Xavier del Bac, 1996.
Helga Teiwes

forty-seven was living either here or in the O'odham community in Tucson and whose family was still at San Xavier in 1802, was its architect/builder. He subsequently applied his skills at Caborca.[108]

After the new temple at San Xavier was ready for use in 1797, Father Llorens directed his attention toward other building projects. One was the Tucson *visita* where he began either a renovation or a replacement for the Garcés chapel. He also proceeded to build a large, two-story adobe *convento*. When it was completed is also unclear, but it was probably after 1804.[109]

His last construction turned out to be the farthest north in the Pimería Alta: the *visita* of Santa Ana de Cuiquiburitac. Situated in the flats just southeast of the Santa Rosa Mountains on the west side of Aguirre Wash and barely beyond the northern boundary of today's Papago Indian Reservation (the home of the Tohono O'odham Nation), the location is presently nothing more than an abandoned archaeological site. Father Llorens wrote in 1811 that he had built "a chapel, an adobe house, and another room that served to shelter the escort and the few laborers with their families whom I had brought here during the past two years." The village continued to be occupied until as late as 1830 before Apaches forced its abandonment. The chapel's copper baptismal font was tossed down a hole that had been dug

for a well and was subsequently excavated in the late nineteenth century after which it was sent to the Smithsonian Institution in Washington, D.C.[110]

All artifacts, by definition, are ideas fashioned into tangible objects. Spanish missions in the Pimería Alta were complex ideas which can be better understood through an appreciation of the monuments they generated. Unfortunately, with but a few exceptions, Jesuit-period constructions have disappeared from the region, along with whatever improvements or replacements the Franciscans may have contributed.[111]

Where there are still cities or towns at former O'odham settlements, as at Ímuris, Santa Cruz, Sáric, Sonoyta, and Tucson, the churches are twentieth-century constructions rather than colonial-period missions. The same is the case in the presidial communities of Tubac, Altar, and Tucson where the old military chapels have disappeared. Tubac is the only one of these former *presidios* with a museum and state park dedicated to telling the story of its past.

The adobe ruins of one other Spanish military post are visible today on the west bank of the San Pedro River within the boundaries

of the San Pedro Riparian National Conservation Area.[112] This was the 1776–1780 location of the wandering *presidio* of Santa Cruz (also known as Terrenate and Santa Cruz de Terrenate) which found its fourth and last home at the present-day town of Santa Cruz, Sonora.

It is our good fortune that all has not been lost through the ravages of time and neglect, and that many Pimería Alta mission monuments, those described herein, remain to be visited and enjoyed.

In spite of the deteriorated condition that by the mid-nineteenth century befell all mission churches across New Spain's former northern borderlands, they became the premier symbol of Spanish presence in the Southwest and have been among the more enduring legacies of that heritage. They are part of the inspiration for architectural styles known as Mission Revival and Santa Fe, or the more eclectic Mediterranean, that have become popular in our own century and, in evolving form, are likely to remain so in the century ahead.

Facing page: **nave and sanctuary, Mission San Ignacio, 1971.**
Joe Baugh

SAINTS, STORIES, AND SACRED PLACES

BY

JAMES S. GRIFFITH

One can't travel far in the Pimería Alta without coming across traces of the Jesuit and Franciscan missionaries who labored for over a century to extend the Spanish Empire and its religion through the desert lands of the north. The eighteenth and nineteenth-century mission churches are the most obvious, but there are many more vestiges: new crops and domestic animals, for instance, that became the staples of this region's economy and diet almost to the present; new stories, replacing the older myths and legends in much of the region; and most especially, a new religion that has left its mark on people and places throughout the Pimería Alta.

Art in the Churches.

One thing that strikes the visitor to a baroque Spanish colonial church in Mexico is an abundance

Facing page: **chapel of Nuestra Señora de los Dolores, Tubutama church, ca. 1975.** Helga Teiwes

of religious art. Statues and paintings representing saints, angels, and members of the Holy Family appear in great profusion on altars and walls. This is true even on the far northwest frontier, the Pimería Alta, where any object of art had either to be created on the spot or carried from some such center as Guadalajara, well over a thousand miles to the south. While mural paintings were by definition executed at the site, the majority of the statues that have survived into the twentieth century appear to have been imported.

Most of these statues are in the baroque style; that is to say, they exemplify the baroque ideals of drama, movement, and richness of material and detail. Rather than standing at rest, many of these figures seem to have been captured in the midst of some sort of action. They appear to be on the verge of moving their arms, or even of stepping off their pedestals. Their faces and hands are finished in an imitation of flesh tones. Their garments are often

covered with small tooled patterns, inlaid with gold leaf. The flesh tone is called *encarnación;* the gold-leaf work, *estofado*. Each was the province of a particular craftsman in some workshop in central Mexico, for these statues were produced, not by single artists, but by teams of specialists. Today, they give eloquent testimony to the high standards of craftsmanship devoted to materials that were to be sent to what for most Mexicans of the time was the end of Nowhere—the region beyond what the historian Herbert Bolton called the Rim of Christendom.

The statues can tell us quite a bit about life at the missions. For instance, almost every church that still has its old statues has a life-size image of the Sorrowing Mother. Such images often consist of finished heads and hands mounted on an armature dressed in real clothes, thus making them easier to carry in processions than fully carved human figures. Another constant figure is the Crucified Christ, often equipped

97

Crucifix in the church of Mission San Francisco del Átil, 1981.
James Officer

Nuestra Señora de los Dolores (Our Mother of Sorrows) in the San Xavier church, ca. 1940.
Edward Ronstadt

with hinged shoulders that allow the body to be removed from the cross, placed in a bier, and paraded around the village.

The presence of these two statues reminds us that a favorite Jesuit missionary teaching tool was the religious drama, and especially the drama of the suffering, death, and resurrection of Jesus. Such Easter season passion plays, with the statues in procession assuming roles in the pageant, once were a regular feature in many of the mission communities of the Pimería Alta. Today, only the Yaqui Indians of southern Arizona, whose aboriginal homelands were in southern Sonora, continue the ancient tradition.

One statue in the Pimería Alta has achieved considerable fame. Lying in state in a side chapel of the nineteenth-century church in Magdalena de Kino is a reclining figure of San Francisco Xavier (Saint Francis Xavier) as his incorrupt body appears in the church of Bom Jesus in the former Portuguese colony of Goa, India. The legend of how the statue came to be in Magdalena, a story that has been told in the Pimería Alta since at least the 1850s, relates that Father Kino ordered the statue for the new church of San Xavier that he was planning to build at the village of Bac, an O'odham community south of Tucson in today's

southern Arizona. When the men carrying the figure arrived in the village at Magdalena, they put it down for a rest. When they tried to pick the statue up, it could not be lifted. This was taken as a miraculous sign that San Francisco desired to remain in Magdalena, and there he stayed.

The reclining figure remained there, in fact, until 1934 when it was removed from the church on orders of the anti-clerical Sonoran state government and burned in the furnaces of the *Cervecería Sonora*, the Sonora Brewery. The statue we see today is a 1940s replacement.

Surrounded by legend and the object of intense regional devotion, this statue has its feast day each year on October 4—not the feast day of San Francisco Xavier at all, which is December 3, but that of San Francisco de Asís, Saint Francis of Assisi, a completely different individual. The statue attracts pilgrims from all over the Pimería Alta to Magdalena, annually swelling the town's population by many thousands of people. Hundreds repay vows to the saint by walking to Magdalena from Nogales or from the even more distant mining town of Cananea, Sonora. Upon arriving in town, the pilgrims stand in line to visit their saint. When they get to the statue, they often lift its head, following a belief that San Francisco will only permit those to do this who are in good standing with him. They may also leave a gift for the saint, often consisting of a *milagro* (miracle), a small metal representation of whatever part of the body needs or has received a miraculous cure.

They then go outside onto Magdalena's two main plazas. These are filled with fiesta-goers, including all those who have come to town to serve the pilgrims' needs: musicians; carnival operators; fortune tellers; and vendors of food and drink, trinkets and toys, pottery, blankets, and herbal medicines. The fiesta even attracts folk artists from nearby Ímuris who sell their handmade, reverse-painted glass frames and boxes, an art form produced nowhere else in northwestern Mexico.

This active involvement of saints and other religious figures in everyday Sonoran life is not limited to Magdalena and its San Francisco. As one drives along Pimería Alta roads, one can see a considerable body of public religious art.

Our Lady of Guadalupe.

Most prominent among the sacred figures depicted in roadside shrines is Our Lady of Guadalupe, the Virgin Mary as she is believed

A holy picture featuring the reclining San Francisco Xavier made by Jesús León for the Magdalena fiesta, 1990.
James Griffith

Mission Santa María Magdalena, 1990. James Officer

Balloons for sale at the Magdalena fiesta, 1968.
James Griffith

to have appeared to a poor Indian outside of Mexico City. Her appearance is said to have occurred in the year 1531, slightly more than a decade after the Spanish conquest of the Valley of Mexico. An Indian named Juan Diego was on his way to Mexico City, the new capital that had risen on the ruins of the Aztec Tenochtitlán. When he came to the hill of Tepeyac, which in Aztec times had been sacred to the mother goddess Tonantzín, he saw a beautiful woman who told him she was the

99

Mother of God and who commanded him to go to see Bishop Zumárraga in Mexico City and tell him that she had requested that a church be built on the spot where she had appeared.

Juan did as he was told, only to be met with a rebuff from the bishop. A second apparition resulted in a second visit and a second refusal. On her third appearance to Juan Diego, the Lady told him to gather roses from the hill and to carry them to the bishop in his *tilma*, or cloak, as proof of her presence. Given that it was winter and freezing cold, there should have been no roses. But Juan found them in bloom, and when he emptied the roses on the floor before the bishop, the image of Our Lady remained on his *tilma*.

It is this *tilma*, believed by many to have been imprinted by the Virgin Mary with her own image, that still hangs in what now is the Basilica of Our Lady of Guadalupe just outside Mexico City. The basilica is the most recent successor of the first church Bishop Zumárraga caused to be built on the site of Juan Diego's vision. It is this image of the Lady, resplendent with sunbeams, cloaked in a starry robe and standing on the crescent moon, that is found all over Mexico—in churches, in homes, on hills, and along the sides of roads.

Shrine dedicated to Nuestra Señora de Guadalupe near Imuris, 1988. James Griffith

Shrine dedicated to Juan Soldado and Nuestra Señora de Guadalupe south of Magdalena, 1987. James Griffith

There are several depictions of Our Lady of Guadalupe along the highways of the Kino Mission Trail. Two are in the old mission town of Ímuris, another is on the highway between Ímuris and Cocóspera, and a fourth is in a road cut just south of Magdalena. Painted by local artists, they serve as objects of contemplation and devotion, reminding their Mexican viewers of their unique relationship with the Mother of God.

Wayside Shrines.

Also found alongside Mexico's highways, as well as next to many roads in southern Arizona, are crosses or small shrines in the form of niches, each marking the spot where someone was killed along the route. This is an old custom in Sonora, one dating back at least to 1783 when the then Bishop of Sonora wrote a letter to Spanish authorities complaining of the tradition which he believed unduly frightened travelers. That his objections had no long-term effect may be seen by driving down any Sonoran highway. The crosses and shrines are there in increasing numbers, reminders of the dangers of travel and the transitory nature of human existence.

Other roadside features are small chapels, often little larger

Music in the Pimería Alta

Music has long been an integral part of life in the Pimería Alta. The O'odham sang, and still sing, in a traditional manner on certain social and religious occasions. Their songs are typically accompanied by gourd rattles, a drum made from an inverted basket, and, sometimes, wood rasps. When missionaries arrived they introduced European instruments and music so there might be suitable accompaniment to Mass and other rituals. Among the instruments they brought were the violin, guitar, and military-style drum—instruments used by present-day O'odham. In the 1750s, Father Ignaz Pfefferkorn, himself an accomplished violinist, mentioned drums, flutes, and guitars as being played by natives and others in Sonora. Sonorans of Hispanic descent still accompany their songs on guitars and violins as well as on a host of more recently introduced instruments.

The best account of late nineteenth century music in the Pimería Alta comes from Luisa Ronstadt Espinel's collection of songs she learned from her father (Linda Ronstadt's grandfather), Federico Ronstadt. Entitled *Canciones de mi Padre*, it contains music and texts for sixteen songs, some of which reflect French influence from the 1860s when French troops occupied Mexico.

Polkas and waltzes have

Mariachis at the Magdalena fiesta, 1968. James Griffith

remained popular since their introduction in the mid-1800s. Many European Americans are surprised to discover that such well-known tunes as "Over the Waves" and the "Jessie Polka" are in fact from nineteenth century Mexico.

Corridos, or story songs, are descended from the old Spanish romances. These home-grown ballads have been popular since the turn of the century, and new ones are constantly being composed. Favorite themes include famous bandits, heroes of the Mexican Revolution, smuggling and immigration incidents, horse races, and tragedies and disasters, including the 1994 assassination of Magdalena-born presidential candidate Luis Donaldo Colosio.

Canciones rancheras are popular songs aimed at a rural or rural-turned-urban audience. They are intensely emotional and deal with such themes as unrequited love,

betrayal, and the alcoholic "cures" for these tragedies. The great *ranchera* composer José Alfredo Jiménez can be compared to United States country music's Hank Williams. Each lived hard, died tragically, and communicated with similar audiences on a deep, heart-rending level.

Two comparatively recent arrivals in the Pimería are *norteña* music, and *mariachi* music. The latter is an import from the Mexican state of Jalisco. Featuring trumpets, violins, and several kinds of guitars, all played by musicians clad in elaborate *charro* costumes, *mariachi* music has changed since the 1920s from a regional folk music to the musical symbol of Mexico. It has been a part of northern Sonora and southern Arizona since the late 1940s.

James S. Griffith

than a telephone booth. Most have been placed and are maintained by families, frequently as a gesture of thanks to one of the saints for a miraculous event. One of these chapels, on the east side of Highway 15 just south of Magdalena, is dedicated to the soul of Juan Soldado, a young recruit in the Mexican army whose real name was Juan Castillo Morales. In 1938 he was stationed in Tijuana, Baja California, when he was accused by his commanding officer of raping and murdering a young girl, a crime the officer himself had committed. This was during a time of serious political riots in Tijuana, and young Juan was swiftly executed by the military authorities.

According to popular belief, however, he started appearing after his death to protest his innocence and began to acquire a reputation for miraculously healing those who appealed to him in prayer. Today there is a large shrine at his grave site in Tijuana filled with offerings of thanksgiving from those who believe he has helped them. His chapel stands on the road between Magdalena and Santa Ana, reminding us that folklore and folk religion remain very much a part of our rapidly changing present.

Saints and members of the Holy Family truly are a daily part of life in the Pimería Alta, as they are all through Catholic Mexico. Not confined to churches, they are to be found by the roadside, in cemeteries, on home altars, and especially in the hearts and memories of the people of this desert land.

More than one community has its story of how a holy personage intervened in its affairs, saving the people from certain disaster. Here are two such legends:

Saint Anthony at Oquitoa.

In the mid-nineteenth century, Oquitoa was besieged by a mixed band of Indians. The outnumbered villagers occupied the church of San Antonio on its mesa, hoping to hold out behind its thick walls. (To this day, Oquitoans can point out where the attackers were gathered in preparation to make the assault.) Suddenly, and for no apparent reason, the Indians dispersed and ran off. Much later, some villagers met one of them and asked why the attack was not pressed home. They were told that when the Indians saw the relief column they knew they had no chance of winning, and ran off. But there had been no relief column, the villagers objected. Oh, yes, they were told. It was a column of cavalry led by a bald-headed officer wearing a gray cloak.

One man who told me this story in the Oquitoa church gestured with his head toward the tonsured, blue-robed statue of San Antonio, Saint Anthony, over the main altar. "It was that guy," he explained. And so to their other legacies from medieval Spain the villagers of Oquitoa add their version of the well-known and widespread legend of a patron saint saving the day by leading a charge against the infidels.

The Virgin Mary at Caborca.

In April of 1857, events got underway which in time would lead to Caborca's official designation "H. Caborca," or "Heroic Caborca," when American adventurer Henry Alexander Crabb led an army of some fifty men overland from San Francisco on what he hoped would mark the first part of a planned conquest of northwest Sonora. After a sharp battle outside of Caborca, the townspeople sought shelter in the mission church of La Purísima Concepción while Crabb and his men occupied a house across the street. In an effort to dislodge the defenders, Crabb and a smaller contingent of his men successfully stormed the convento wing attached to the church on its north side. After an ineffective attempt to use a keg of powder to blow in the door between the convento and the church's north sacristy, Crabb retreated from the convento to the house and he and his followers settled down to a siege lasting several days.

The stalemate was ended when a relief column of Mexican soldiers arrived. A flaming arrow shot by a Papago ignited the roof of Crabb's house of refuge, and the filibuster and his army surrendered on April 6 (today the name of the street leading to the mission is Calle 6 de Abril). All but sixteen-year-old Charles Edward Evans, who was spared because of his youth, were summarily executed. Crabb's head was cut off and kept as a trophy in an earthenware jar filled with vinegar. The Evans boy was allowed to return to California where he wrote an account of the expedition and its fate.[113] (One of the important roles played on the Mexican side in the drama was that of José María Redondo, who in 1857 was Prefect of the District of Altar in which Caborca was located. He is a direct ancestor of the well-known American singer, Linda Ronstadt.[114])

So much for documentary history. Regional tradition, preserved in at least one Sonoran family, tells us a bit more. When Charley Evans was taken prisoner, he had put one question to his captors: "Who was that lady?"

Upon perceiving that no one knew what he meant, he explained. When Crabb and his men lit the fuse of the keg that was to blow in the sacristy door, they retired to a safe place to await the explosion. Before it could occur, a lady in blue appeared by the keg and put out the fuse. The attackers tried again and again, this time with sharpshooters ready to gun down the brave woman. But each time she appeared and extinguished the burning fuse, she remained untouched by bullets.

The church at Caborca is dedicated to La Purísima Concepción de Nuestra Señora, the Immaculate Conception of the Virgin Mary. Her image at Caborca is dressed in blue, and she is thus credited by some with having intervened to save her building and people. The narrative has apparently been preserved in a family context ever since Henry Alexander Crabb's defeat and execution, to be made public only within the past few years.

Churches, roadside shrines and crosses, stories, pilgrimages—all are evidence that the cultural and religious systems introduced into the Pimería Alta by Eusebio Francisco Kino and his successors are alive and have flourished for more than three centuries. It is not so much that the land is filled with Catholic churches, many of which

date from the days of New Spain, nor that Mass is still said in most of these colonial buildings. More important is the existence of a rich tradition of folk Catholicism in the minds, hearts, and memories of the people of the Pimería, a body of informal legacies in which we can share every time we drive the highways, visit with villagers, or stroll around the plaza at Magdalena. Unique to the region in their details, yet tied to the rest of Mexico and, indeed, to Spain in their general patterns, these religious traditions add beauty and excitement to any journey along the Kino Trail.

Interior of a chapel dedicated to Juan Soldado, south of Magdalena, 1991. James Griffith

WOMEN, FAITH, AND FAMILY

BY
CARMEN VILLA DE PREZELSKI

As it is with much of what has been written about the cultures of the world, the contribution of the women of Sonora has been largely ignored in the written word. But for centuries the women who live here have learned, and then passed along to their daughters and granddaughters, a way of life that makes Sonora—and its Pimería Alta—a place like no other.

A Woman's Realm.

If a husband must travel far to earn a living, it is a wife who must, through her quiet strength, keep the family together. When the children or the elderly take sick, it is the women who rely on centuries-old knowledge of healing and care-giving to make things right again.

In the absence of the availability of more formal instruction, women have passed along to

Facing page: Doña Juana Sepulveda at home, Ejido de Coyotillo, near Santa Ana, 1994.
David Burckhalter

their children the doctrines of the Catholic church. Women, banding together in committees, organize fiestas, see to the maintenance of churches and other public buildings, and support the schools.

The food of Sonora reflects both its history and environment. Beginning in the late seventeenth century, Spaniards introduced beef, dairy products, and wheat to the area. Many of Sonora's traditional recipes include some or all of these basic products. Flour tortillas have become popular all over Mexico but they originated here, in northern Sonora. But while the ingredients might be European in origin, the dishes decidedly are influenced by native cultures and arid climate.

Maize, a plant native only to the New World, used as kernels or ground into *masa*, is a component of many traditional foods. Cacti, agaves, and other desert plants are used both as food and medicine. The chile pepper, also a New World native, is in its many varieties and various stages—raw, cooked, or

dried—a seemingly ubiquitous element in Sonoran dishes.

Food is fundamental to a people's cultural memory. It is often the reason, or the excuse, for members of communities to come together in public places. It also affords a reason for the family to gather around a kitchen table where many of the family's values are subtly passed along on a daily basis. Holidays, those signposts that mark what is most important to a culture, are forever connected to certain foods.

In Sonora, it is almost always the women who prepare the food. The present-day woman who has written the "diary" you are about to read is fictional. She has been invented to provide a glimpse into the daily life of a small Pimería Alta town. She does not exist, yet she is everywhere in the Sonoran countryside.

A Pimería Alta Year.

January 5—The day is still young but I have accomplished much already. We met at the church this morning, my neighbors and I, to clean and to put new paper flowers on the altars. This winter has been cold and the gardens have all frozen. No fresh flowers anywhere. Still, the church will look very pretty for the Epiphany tomorrow. Right now I must go find the mayor, the Presidente Municipal, so that he will send me some men to clean the plaza in front of the church. I have to hurry home and do some cooking tonight or my family will have no tamales with which to celebrate the coming of the Three Kings.

January 6—Doña Chu, the oldest lady in town, continues to feel sick. I visited her today and tried to get her to eat. She would only drink some camomile tea and took three small bites from a tortilla. Doña Chu (her real name is María Jesús) used to make the best tortillas in town. I remember when I was a little girl I would spend my mornings with her so that I could witness the miracle of her stretching that little ball of *masa*, made from wheat flour, shortening, and water, into great big tortillas, more than two feet across—so big that each one took up the whole comal, or griddle, on which she cooked them over a fire in her yard.

March 1—The parish mothers and

their teen-aged daughters met today to begin organizing the catechism class for the children. There will be several making their First Holy Communion this spring.

March 10—Will Lent ever end? We keep up the old ways here. For forty days there are no parties at people's homes, no weddings in the church, and no dances held in the *casino*, the town social hall. It used to be that no one ate meat during Lent; now the Holy Father says that we only need to keep meatless Fridays. But not here. We still keep Lent the old-fashioned way. Believe me, for Sonoran people to give up meat, especially beef, is a real sacrifice. Toward the end of the season, it is difficult for me to come up with ideas for meatless dishes that will satisfy the family.

March 26—Today my mother, Doña Mati everyone calls her, has finally finished the girls' Easter dresses. She has not lost her touch for sewing or cooking. She used to live down the street from us, but when father died, she gave her house to my brother and his wife and moved in with us. She helps me a lot around the house. I am happy to have her with us. All the old people in town live with their families. Why should they be alone with relatives so nearby?

Papa has been dead for twelve years but Mama still wears only black clothes, *luto* we call it, because she is still in mourning for him.

March 27—Beto, my husband Roberto, wove little crosses from the palm leaves that the children brought home after Palm Sunday Mass. We will put the crosses over the doors of the house so that they will protect us against lightning during the summer storms.

April 3—The Easter Mass was very nice. The altars were decorated with larkspur and hollyhock collected from various gardens in town. On my way home from the church, I could hear a radio playing in each house as I passed the open doors. After forty very quiet days, we can have music again. I had to hurry home to check on the lunch I left cooking on the stove. Our Easter meal was a *cocido*: potatoes, onions, and other vegetables simmered for a long time with beef. After all this time, finally, beef again.

May 5—Today is a national holiday because on this day in 1862, the Mexican army defeated the French army. I understand it is celebrated in the United States but we do not make much of it here.

May 10—I know that Mother's Day in the United States moves around, but in Mexico, it is always on the tenth of May. Beto was gone all day because he drove to the ranch where he was born to put flowers on his mother's grave. His parents worked all their lives for the same rancher and now the two of them are buried there on his land. I am so grateful to still be able to celebrate the day with my mother. I prepared one of her favorite dishes for our supper, *pollo con pipián*, pieces of chicken in a thick red chile sauce.

May 15—Six children from the town made their First Communion today. None of my children was involved. The two older ones already have done it and the youngest is not ready yet.

After the Mass there were two baptisms. Beto and I were *padrino* and *madrina*, or godparents, for one beautiful baby girl. Now this little girl will call us her *niños*. Being *niños* is a great responsibility. If anything should happen to Dolores and Pepe, we will be responsible for a proper and religious upbringing of their daughter. From now on Dolores, Pepe, Beto, and I will call each other *compadre* and *comadre*. It is as if they have become our brother and sister, and their whole family, not just their baby, is now our family.

Preparing the noon meal, Sonora, **1993.** David Burckhalter

At work in the kitchen, Sonora, 1993. David Burckhalter

Making empanadas, Sonora, 1993. David Burckhalter

As our first duty as godparents Beto and I hosted a party in our backyard. We grilled strips of beef over hot coals, *carne asada* we call it, and then served it in gorditas. These small, thick flour tortillas are just right for holding lots of meat and plenty of green chile salsa.

May 22—Beto and our boy went out to the desert today to harvest the tender new pads of the *nopal*, or prickly pear cactus. Once we burn off the thorns, we slice the *nopales* into thin strips and cook them. They taste something like green beans.

June 1—Today marks the end of the weekly meetings and the beginning of the daily meetings for the committee that is planning the town's fiesta for Día de San Juan. Some of the women on the committee can be difficult, but the rest of us just work around them. There is much to do. The plaza must be cleaned and decorated. Our fiesta is famous and people come from miles around. We hope to make lots of money from the dance. The church roof and floor need repairs, and this year we hope to finally have enough money to build a shelter at the place by the highway where the school bus picks up the children.

June 24—Día de San Juan, the feast of Saint John the Baptist. Early in the morning, all of us went down to the river, took off our shoes, and waded in the water. Even Mama! I think she went in the water because that was the only way she could make sure all of us poured a little water on our heads. Mama believes that if you wet your feet and do not also wet your head, you catch cold.

We have not had a chance to count the money yet, but the dance was a big success. The sales of the green corn tamales, which we made with plenty of cheese and green chile, went very well. The committee was lucky to get

one of the most popular *Norteña* bands in Sonora to play at the dance. One of the musicians played a button accordion, and others played a twelve-stringed bass guitar, a saxophone, a stand-up bass fiddle, and a snare drum. They played polkas and waltzes as well as the bolero and cumbia. The musicians in this *conjunto*, as such bands are called, dressed in the clothes of *vaqueros*: Stetson hat, western pants and shirt, and cowboy boots.

This famous *conjunto* drew a much bigger crowd than the group we had last year. During breaks, the dancers sat at the little metal tables provided for us by the beer company, drinking beer or soft drinks and, I am happy to report, eating lots of tamales. The beer company gets all the money from drink sales but we get the *tamal* money.

San Juan was good to us in every way but one. It did not rain today. Beto has planted corn and squash this year and, of course, there are always the fruit trees. I hope the saint sends rain soon.

June 26—Every year many of the people who have moved away from our little town come back during the Fiesta de San Juan for a sort of homecoming which we call *Caravana de Recuerdo*. My own cousin and his family, who live in

Phoenix now, came to visit my aunt and uncle. For days, almost every house had a car with an Arizona or California license plate parked in front of it. But now they are all gone.

July 21—Last night I made *chilaquiles* (cut up corn tortillas and cheese in red chile sauce), and they were a real disappointment. I went to Doña Juanita at the store to tell her so. I will not buy cheese from her anymore if the quality does not improve. After all, a good cheese should string, not lump, when it melts.

September 12—School started today for our two older children. I worry about them. At least when they are with me, I know they are eating well. I make a *caldo*, a nice pot of soup, everyday for lunch. But when they are gone all day, who knows what they are eating. At least the baby is still at home with me.

October 28—My *comadre* María came over today to help me make the *membrilla*, the quince candy for which our town is famous. It is especially good served with little slices of *queso fresco*, a white cheese similar to farmer's cheese.

November 2—For several days, people who grew up here but have moved away, many to the United States, have been coming into town. They have come to look after the graves in which their family members are buried. It is an obligation that is taken very seriously, but the fulfillment of that obligation varies from town to town. In some places, this observance of *El Día de los Muertos*—the Day of the Dead, or All Souls' Day—is a very solemn occasion, while in others it is almost a fiesta. With us, it is a little bit of both.

Last night, families prayed rosaries at graves while hundreds of candles flickered in the dark. This morning at dawn, the cemetery was carpeted with golden and orange marigolds that the people had scattered.

At the gate to the cemetery, there were booths where flowers and food were for sale. Most of the booths were selling *aguas frescas*, various kinds of traditional liquid refreshments: *jamaica*, made from hibiscus blossoms; *tamarindo*, from pods of a tree that grows in the south where it rains a lot; and *horchata*, made from rice water and flavored with almonds. These days, most of the children seem to prefer bottled soft drinks, even as many prefer packaged white bread over tortillas.

December 24—Christmas Eve, *Noche Buena*, or the Good Night. When

Making tortillas, Sonora, 1995.
David Burckhalter

my mother was young, Christmas was mostly a religious holiday in Mexico and not such a family celebration. Now Christmas and Christmas Eve mean gifts and even decorated trees. I think that we must have borrowed all of this from the United States.

December 31—Tonight we will build a big fire in the backyard and wait for the New Year. We will talk about the old days with Mama, tell silly stories, look at the stars, and eat fried pork rinds, which we call *chicharrones*, with plenty of the red chile and vinegar salsa that we buy in the little bottles at the store.

It has been a good year.

APPENDIX I
Identifying Saints in the Pimería Alta

BY
JAMES S. GRIFFITH

Christ (*Cristo*): He is commonly represented as he stood before Pontius Pilot (*El Nazareno*), suffered on the road to Calvary (*Camino al Calvario*), suffered on the cross (*La Crucifixión*), or as he lay entombed (*Entierro de Cristo*). He also appears as a child in Nativity scenes as well as in two special manifestations: the Holy Child of Prague (*Santo Niño de Praga*), in which he sits crowned, holding an orb of the world; and the Holy Child of Atocha (*Santo Niño de Atocha*), a particularly Mexican manifestation in which he is also seated, but clad as a pilgrim in cloak and broad hat, carrying a staff and gourd canteen.

The Virgin Mary (*La Virgen* or *Nuestra Señora*). She appears most often as the Immaculate Conception (*La Inmaculada* or *La Purísima Concepción*; feast day, December 8) and the Sorrowing Mother (*La Dolorosa*; feast day, September 15). She is also omnipresent as the

Virgin of Guadalupe (*Nuestra Señora de Guadalupe*; feast day, December 12). As the Immaculate Conception, she is patroness of Caborca and, possibly, of Tumacácori in its last months. As Holy Mary of the People (*Santa María del Pópulo*), she is patroness of Bísanig.

Saint Anthony of Padua (*San Antonio de Padua*; 1195–1231). His image is that of a tonsured Franciscan wearing a blue or dark brown habit, often holding an image of the Christ child as well as a stalk of lilies or a staff. He was a powerful Franciscan preacher and worker of miracles. Patron of the poor and oppressed, he is also invoked against infertility and by those seeking the return of lost articles. Patron of Oquitoa, his feast day is June 13.

Saint Didacus (*San Diego de Alcalá*; 1400–1463). Didacus was a Spanish-born Franciscan brother noted for his healing powers and miracles. The cross, roses, and bread are his attributes. His intercession was credited by King Philip II of Spain with having cured his son. Patron of cooks; San Diego, California; and of Pitiquito, his feast day is November 13.

Saint Francis of Assisi (*San Francisco de Asís*; 1181–1226). He typically appears wearing a grey or

brown habit, often holding a skull or crucifix. He is also depicted kneeling while receiving the Holy Stigmata or five wounds of Christ. Founder of the Order of Friars Minor, this Italian-born brother is invoked against fire and is patron of animals, ecology, tapestry makers, Italy, and Átil. His feast day is October 4.

Saint Francis Xavier (*San Francisco Xavier*; 1506–1552). Dressed in a black cassock and shown either reclining, as a corpse (rarely except in the Pimería Alta), or preaching while holding a crucifix, Xavier, the Basque Apostle to the Indies, was one of the original followers of fellow Basque, Saint Ignatius (*San Ignacio*), founder of the Jesuits. He is patron of foreign missions, tourism, Goa, Outer Mongolia, India, Japan, and San Xavier del Bac. His feast day is December 3.

Saint James the Greater (*Santiago de Compostela* or *Santiago Matamoros*; first century). Shown as a pilgrim, in supplication to the Virgin Mary, standing on a jasper pillar, or on horseback killing Moors (*Matamoros* means Moor Slayer), the Apostle James the Greater is symbolized by a cockleshell or pilgrim's hat. He is said to have preached in Spain and his body is believed to be buried in Compostela. He is patron of veterinarians, horsemen, laborers, furriers, soldiers, Spain, Guatemala, Nicaragua, the militant expansion of Spanish Catholicism, and is invoked against arthritis and rheumatism. With Our Lady of the Pillar, he is patron of Cocóspera. His feast day is July 25.

Saint Ignatius of Loyola (*San Ignacio de Loyola*; 1491?–1556). Founder of the Society of Jesus (the Jesuits), a Basque, he often appears as a bald, bearded man in a black cassock, frequently holding a book. Invoked by persons suffering from overly delicate conscience, he is patron of retreats, spiritual exercises, and San Ignacio de Cabórica. His feast day is July 31.

Saint Isidore (*San Ysidro*; died 1130). Shown praying while an angel plows for him, Isidore was an exemplary Christian who shared his food with the poor. Born near Madrid, this Spanish favorite is patron of farmers, farm workers, and ranchers. Rather than in the churches of the Pimería Alta, San Ysidro appears mainly on altars in its homes and in the hearts of those who work the land. His feast day is May 15.

Saint Joseph (*San José*). Husband of the Virgin Mary, he is depicted as a bearded man, usually holding a lily and the Christ child. Invoked

against communism and doubt, he is patron of carpenters, fathers, happy death, house hunting, laborers, Austria, Belgium, Canada, Mexico, Peru, Vietnam, Ímuris, and, after 1753, Tumacácori. His feast day is March 19.

Saint Lucy (*Santa Lucía*; fourth century). She is often shown holding a dish containing a pair of eyes. This Sicilian virgin and martyr is patroness of gondoliers, glaziers, cutlers, and lamplighters and is invoked against eye disease, throat infections, hemorrhage, and dysentery. Her feast day is December 13.

Saint Mary Magdalene (*Santa María Magdalena*; first century). Shown in religious imagery as a young woman with long hair and humbly clad, Mary Magdalene, a reformed harlot and "sinner with seven devils," was the first to see and recognize the Risen Saviour. She is patroness of contemplatives, fallen women, glovers, hairdressers, perfumers, and Magdalena de Kino. Her feast day is July 22.

Saint Martin of Porres (*San Martín de Porres*; 1579–1639). A lay brother, he is seen wearing a Dominican habit, often holding a broom and with a cat near his feet. The Peruvian son of a Spanish knight and black Panamanian freedwoman, this self-proclaimed

Brother Broom or Mulatto Dog cared for slaves, orphans, dogs and cats, sick people, and even rats and mice. He is the patron of social justice, public health workers, public education, hairdressers, persons of mixed race, persons in the lowest rungs of the social and economic ladder, and Peruvian television. His feast day is November 3.

Saints Peter and Paul (*San Pedro y San Pablo*; first century). Both are seen in religious imagery with white beards. Peter holds the keys to heaven and is also symbolized by a rooster, fish, or ship. He was one of the Twelve Apostles and the first Bishop of Rome. Peter is patron of boatwrights, clock makers, fishermen, and net makers, and is invoked against fever, foot trouble, and wolves.

Paul's chief emblems are a sword and a book. He was a converted persecutor of Christians and letter writer of the early church. Paul is patron of rope makers, tent makers, upholsterers, the Cursillo Movement, Greece, and Malta.

Jointly, they are Patrons of Tubutama, and they share June 29 as their feast day.

James S. Griffith

APPENDIX II

Elevations above Sea Level
and Populations of Selected Sites
in the Pimería Alta

Site	Elevation in feet	Population in 1990
Ajo, AZ	1,800	2,919
Altar, SON	1,302	6,458
Átil, SON	1,886	797
Caborca, SON	950	59,160
Casa Grande, AZ	1,400	19,082
Cocóspera, SON	3,600	—
Ímuris, SON	2,515	7,365
Magdalena de Kino, SON	2,493	20,071
Nogales, AZ	3,700	21,000
Nogales, SON	3,700	107,936
Oquitoa, SON	1,700	424
Pitiquito, SON	1,083	7,743
Presa Cuauhtemoc, SON	1,936	—
Puerto Peñasco, SON	40	26,675
Quitovac, SON	1,148	54
Santa Ana, SON	2,230	12,745
Santa Teresa, SON	1,750	—
Sells, AZ	2,404	2,750
Sonoyta, SON	1,289	9,728
Trincheras, SON	1,800	2,109
Tubutama, SON	2,000	1,842
Tucson, AZ	2,400	433,300
Tumacacori, AZ	3,250	250

NOTES

1. Bringas (1977: 25).

2. Burrus (1971: 430). Translation by Thomas Sheridan.

3. Atondo Rodríguez and Ortega Soto (1985: 79); Polzer (1972: 258–259); Schroeder (1956: 103, 108–109 n. 8). For an overview of Sonoran missions, see Eckhart and Griffith (1975).

4. Nentvig (1980: 109); Pfefferkorn (1989: 79–80).

5. Pfefferkorn (1989: 272–273).

6. Manje (1954: 78, 82, 93, 110, 115, 144, 167).

7. Nentvig (1980: 69).

8. Kino (1948: II: 168–169).

9. Burrus and Zubillaga (1982: 148).

10. Pfefferkorn (1989: 79–80).

11. Kelemen (1977: 107–108); Ruiz (1965).

12. Pfefferkorn (1989: 80).

13. Eckhart and Griffith (1975: 76–78); Roca (1967: 156).

14. Carlisle and Fontana (1969: 183 n. 58); McCarty (1981: 50–51).

15. Almada (1952: 513–514); Stagg (1976: 67, 81).

16. Almada (1952: 701–702).

17. McCarty (1981: 44–49); Reyes (1772: 48–59).

18. McCarty (1981: 90).

19. McCarty (1973: 92–93).

20. Reyes (1772: 46).

21. Barbastro (1971: 61–62). Translation by Daniel S. Matson.

22. Font (1930); Garcés (1900; 1965); Kessell (1970: 183); McCarty (1981: 49); Roca (1967: 362 n. 57).

23. McCarty (1981: 65); Reyes (1772: 56); Roca (1967: 102–104, 106–107); Sedelmayr (1747).

24. Barbastro (1971: 75). Translation here by Kieran R. McCarty.

25. Bringas (1977: 59 n. 26, 139 n. 112).

26. Barbastro (1971: 80); translation by Daniel S. Matson.

27. Roca (1967: 108–110).
28. Sedelmayr (1747).
29. Barbastro (1788); Reyes (1772: 56–57); Yturralde (1797).
30. Kino (1971: 87)
31. Roca (1967: 109–110).
32. Kessell (1976: 201, 247); Roca (1967: 112).
33. Barbastro (1788); Yturralde (1797).
34. Reyes (1772: 59); Roca (1967: 116–117).
35. Bringas (1977: 59 *n.* 26, 108 *n.* 90, 145); Font (1975: 265).
36. Yturralde (1797).
37. Roca (1967: 118–119).
38. Roca (1967: 119–120).
39. Reyes (1772: 58).
40. Barbastro (1788; 1971: 61–62 *n.* 14).
41. Roca (1967: 120); Yturralde (1797).
42. Baldonado (1959); Bringas (1977: 59 *n.* 26).
43. Archivo Iglesias Parroquiales . . . ; Noticias . . . (1803–1804); Schuetz–Miller (1993: 298).
44. Goss (1975: 175, 177–178).
45. Bleser (1993); Pickens (1993: 176 *n.* 5).
46. Roca (1967: 122–123).
47. Reyes (1772: 59); Roca (1967: 123).
48. Bringas (1977: 143, 146–147, 150); Yturralde (1797).
49. Noticias . . . (1803–1804); Pickens (1993: 107–111); Roca (1967: 123).
50. Kino (1948: I: 115–116; II: 110). The story of Nuestra Señora del Pilar y Santiago is told by Simmons (1991: 35).
51. Roca (1967: 85).
52. Roca (1967: 85–86).
53. Kino (1948: II: 86–88).
54. Davis and Goss (1977: 26).
55. Sedelmayr (1751).
56. Reyes (1772: 51); Roca (1967: 87).
57. Davis and Goss (1977: 27–28, 33).
58. Davis and Goss (1977: 28).

59. Bartlett (1965: I: 413–414).
60. Bartlett (1965: I: 472); Wyllys (1932: 63–64, 95–96, 105).
61. Browne (1951: 181–182).
62. Officer (1984).
63. Reyes (1772: 53); Roca (1967: 56–57).
64. Bartlett (1965: I: 418); Stern and Jackson (1988: 472).
65. Borhegyi (1956: 1–4).
66. Officer (1987: 73–74, 168–169, 370 *n.* 44); Williams (1986b: 122).
67. Kino (1971: 136–139).
68. Roca (1967: 58–60). The story of Father Campos is related by Dunne (1941).
69. Roca (1967: 60).
70. Reyes (1772: 52–53).
71. Bringas (1977: 59 *n.* 26); Roca (1967: 59–61).
72. Kessell (1970: 157).
73. Roca (1967: 64).
74. Reyes (1772: 54); Roca (1967: 64).
75. Font (1975: 273–274).
76. Yturralde (1797).
77. Bartlett (1965: I: 431); Browne (1951: 173); Eckhart and Griffith (1975: 27).
78. Polzer (1982: 35, 62).
79. Font (1930: 13–14); Reyes (1772: 52); Stern and Jackson (1988: 471).
80. Kessell (1970: 48–49).
81. Kino (1948: II: 303, 307).
82. Kessell (1970: 31, 36, 48).
83. Kessell (1970: 51).
84. Kessell (1970: 100, 102).
85. Burton (1992a, 1992b); Pickens (1993: 138–139); Robinson (1976); Stoner (1937).
86. Kessell (1970: 132, 136).
87. Reyes (1772: 49–50).
88. Kessell (1976: 57, 88).
89. Manje (1954: 94, 168).
90. Bleser (n.d.: 15–16); Kessell (1970: 144).
91. Moyano (1803; 1807).
92. Liberós (1822; 1823).
93. Bleser (n.d.: 20–21, 26–31).

94. Kessell (1970: 143–144).
95. Kessell (1970: 153, 201; 1976: 73 *n.* 18).
96. Kessell (1976: 130).
97. Fontana (1971: 74); Kessell (1976: 239, 283).
98. Fontana (1971: 75–77).
99. Fontana (1971: 80–81, 83).
100. Fontana (1961: 2, 4); Sedelmayr (1751).
101. Fontana (1961: 7); Reyes (1772: 48). Structural details were revealed in archaeology carried out at the site of the Espinosa church (Cheek 1974; Robinson 1963).
102. Williams (1986b: 117); Yturralde (1797).
103. Schaefer, Chinn, and McCarty (1977: 44).
104. Barbastro (1788); Schaefer, Chinn, and McCarty (1977: 45).
105. Kessell (1976: 159); Schaefer, Chinn, and McCarty (1977: 44).
106. Schaefer, Chinn, and McCarty (1977: 47, 49).
107. The indication of the later removal and re-use is archaeological as well as based on other physical evidence. Similarly, the interior stone rubble core between the brick walls was discovered by workers repairing the building in 1989.
108. Archivo Iglesias Parroquiales Sonora, Caborca; Census. 1802; Fontana (1961: 11); Padrones . . . (1801).
109. Williams (1986b: 120–121).
110. Ahlborn (1987); Fontana (1987).
111. Summaries of the histories for each of these places, except for Sonoita, Arizona, are in Roca (1967).
112. Williams (1986a).
113. The most complete account in English of the Crabb filibustering expedition is by Robert H. Forbes (1952). The most complete version in Spanish is by Ruibal Corella (1976).
114. An excellent account of the Ronstadt family's connections to the Pimería Alta is in Ronstadt (1993).

BIBLIOGRAPHY

The following list includes works cited in the notes as well as other sources of information not so identified.

Ahlborn, Richard E.
1987b   An Arizona Mission Font: Research Note to Fontana's "Santa Ana de Cuiquiburitac." *Journal of the Southwest*, Vol. 29, no. 2 (Summer), pp. 160–163. Tucson, University of Arizona Press and the Southwest Center.

Alcock, John
1985   *Sonoran Desert Spring.* Chicago, The University of Chicago Press.
1990   *Sonoran Desert Summer.* Tucson, The University of Arizona Press.

Almada, Francisco R.
1952   *Diccionario de Historia, Geografía y Biografía Sonorenses.* Chihuahua, Impresora Ruíz Sandoval.

Archivo Iglesias Parroquiales. Sonora. Caborca. Film no. 0552.1, Arizona Historical Society, Tucson.

Atondo Rodríguez, Ana María, and Martha Ortega Soto
1985   Entrada de colonos españoles en Sonora durante el siglo XVII. In *Historia General de Sonora,* edited by Sergio Ortega Noriega and Ignacio del Río Vol. 2, *De la Conquista al Estado Libre y Soberano de Sonora,* pp. 77–110. Hermosillo, Gobierno del Estado de Sonora.

Bahr, Donald, Juan Gregorio, David I. López, and Albert Alvarez
1974   *Piman Shamanism and Staying Sickness (Ká:cim Múmkidag).* Tucson, The University of Arizona Press.

Baldonado, Luis
1959   The dedication of Caborca. *The Kiva,* Vol. 24, no. 4 (April), inside back cover. Tucson, Arizona Archaeological and Historical Society.

Barbastro, Francisco A.
1788   "Compendio de los más notable que han trabajado en Sonora los hijos del Colegio de la Santa Cruz, 1768–1783, Babiácora, Sept. 10." Unpublished. Original in the Fr. Marcellino da Civezza Collection, 202.35, Antonianum Library, Rome. Microfilm 305 in the University of Arizona Library, Tucson. Typescript copy provided by Kieran R. McCarty.
1971   *Sonora hacia fines del siglo XVIII. Un informe del misionero franciscano Fray Francisco Antonio Barbastro, con otros documentos complementarios.* [*Documentación Histórica Mexicana,* Vol. 3.] Edited and annotated by Lino Gómez Canedo. Guadalajara, Librería Font, S.A.

Barnes, Thomas C., Thomas H. Naylor, and Charles W. Polzer
1981   *Northern New Spain: A Research Guide.* Tucson, The University of Arizona Press.

Bartlett, John R.
1965   *Personal Narrative of Explorations in Texas, New Mexico, California, Sonora, and Chihuahua.* Two volumes. Chicago, The Rio Grande Press, Inc.

Bleser, Nicholas J.
1993   Caborca alert! *SMRC-Newsletter,* Vol. 27, no. 94 (March), pp. 1–4. Tucson, Southwestern Mission Research Center.
n.d.   *Tumacacori: From Ranchería to National Monument.* Tucson, Southwest Parks and Monuments Association.

Bolton, Herbert E.
1984   *Rim of Christendom: A Biography of Eusebio Francisco Kino, Pacific Coast Pioneer.* Re-edition, with a new foreword by John L. Kessell. Tucson, The University of Arizona Press.
1986   *The Padre on Horseback: A Sketch of Eusebio Francisco Kino, S.J., Apostle to the Pimas.* Re-edition. Chicago, Loyola University Press.

Borhegyi, Stephen F. de
1956   *El Santuario de Chimayo.* [Santa Fe], Spanish Colonial Arts Society, Inc.

Bringas de Manzaneda y Encinas, Diego Miguel
1977   *Friar Bringas Reports to the King: Methods of Indoctrination on the Frontier of New Spain 1796–97.* Translated and edited by Daniel S. Matson and Bernard L. Fontana. Tucson, The University of Arizona Press.

Brown, David E., *editor*
1982   Biotic Communities of the American Southwest— United States and Mexico. *Desert Plants,* Vol. 4, nos. 1–4, pp. 1–342. Superior, Arizona, The University of Arizona for the Boyce Thompson Arboretum.

Browne, John R.
1951   *A Tour Through Arizona, 1864, or Adventures in the Apache Country.* Tucson, Arizona Silhouettes.

Burrus, Ernest J.
1971   *Kino and Manje: Explorers of Sonora and Arizona, Their Vision of the Future. A Study of Their Expeditions and Plans.* [*Sources and Studies for the History of the Americas,* Vol. 10.] Rome, Italy, and St. Louis, Missouri, Jesuit Historical Institute.

Burrus, Ernest J., and Félix Zubillaga
1982   *Misiones Mexicanas de la Compañía de Jesús, 1618-1745.* Madrid, Ediciones José Porrúa Turanzas.

Burton, Geoffrey F.
1992a   Remnants of Adobe and Stone: The Surface Archeology of the Guevavi and Calabazas Units, Tumacacori National Historical Park, Arizona. *Publications in Anthropology,* no. 59. Tucson, Western Archeological and Conservation Center, National Park Service, U.S. Department of the Interior.
1992b   San Miguel de Guevavi: The Archeology of an Eighteenth Century Jesuit Mission on the Rim of Christendom. *Publications in Anthropology,* no. 57. Tucson, Western Archeological and Conservation Center, National Park Service, U.S. Department of the Interior.

Cabot, Erni; Charles W. Polzer, S.J.; and Carmen Villa de Prezelski
1982–   *Father Eusebio Francisco Kino And His Missions of the*
1983   *Pimería Alta, Book 1: The Side Altars; Book 2: The Main Altars; Book 3: Facing The Missions.* Southwestern Mission Research Center, Tucson, Arizona.

Carlisle, Charles R., *translator,* and Bernard L. Fontana, *editor*
1969   Sonora in 1773. Reports by Five Jaliscan Friars. Parts I and II. *Arizona and the West,* Vol. 11, no. 1 (Spring), pp. 39-56, and no. 2 (Summer), pp. 179–190. Tucson, The University of Arizona Press.

Census. 1802. 18th Century Selected Parish Archives #1. Dobyns' Project, Arizona Historical Society, Tucson.

Cheek, Annette L.
1974   "The Evidence for Acculturation in Artifacts: Indians and Non-Indians at San Xavier del Bac, Arizona." Unpublished Ph.D. dissertation, The University of Arizona, Tucson.

Chronic, Halka
1983   *Roadside Geology of Arizona.* Missoula, Mountain Press Publ. Co.

Crosby, Alfred
1972   *The Columbian Exchange: Biological and Cultural Consequences of 1492.* Westport, Greenwood Press.

Davis, Natalie Y., and Robert C. Goss
1977   Cocóspera: Lonely Sentinel of Resurrection. *El Palacio,* Vol. 83, no. 2 (Summer), pp. 24–43. Santa Fe, Museum of New Mexico.

Delaney, John I.
1980   *Dictionary of Saints.* Garden City, New York, Doubleday.

Dobyns, Henry F.
1976   *Spanish Colonial Tucson: A Demographic History.* Tucson, The University of Arizona Press.

Dunne, Peter M.
1941   Captain Anza and the Case of Father Campos. *Mid-America,* Vol. 23, no. 1 (January), pp. 45–60. Chicago, Loyola University.

Eckhart, George B., and James S. Griffith
1975   *Temples in the Wilderness.* Tucson, Arizona Historical Society.

Espinel, Luisa
1946   Canciones De Mi Padre. Spanish Folksongs from Southern Arizona. *University of Arizona Bulletin,* vol. 17, no. 1. [*General Bulletin,* no. 10.] Tucson, University of Arizona.

Ezell, Paul H.
1961   *The Hispanic Acculturation of the Gila River Pimas.* [*Memoirs of the American Anthropological Association,* no. 90.] Menasha, Wisconsin, American Anthropological Association.

Font, Pedro
1930   *Font's Complete Diary of the Second Anza Expedition.* [*Anza's California Expeditions,* Vol. 4.] Translated and edited by Herbert E. Bolton. Berkeley, University of California Press.
1975   Letters of Friar Pedro Font, 1776–1777. Translated by Daniel S. Matson; introduction by Lora L. Miller. *Ethnohistory,* Vol. 22, no. 3 (Summer), pp. 263–293. Tucson, American Society for Ethnohistory.

Fontana, Bernard L.
1961   Biography of a Desert Church: The Story of Mission San Xavier del Bac. *The Smoke Signal,*

no. 3 (Spring), pp. 1–24. Tucson, Tucson Corral of the Westerners.

1971 Calabazas of the Río Rico. *The Smoke Signal*, no. 24 (Fall), pp. 65–88. Tucson, Tucson Corral of the Westerners.

1987 Santa Ana de Cuiquiburitac: Pimería Alta's Northernmost Mission. Translations by Daniel S. Matson. *Journal of the Southwest*, Vol. 29, no. 2 (Summer), pp. 133–159. Tucson, University of Arizona Press and the Southwest Center.

1989 *Of Earth and Little Rain: The Papago Indians*. Photography by John P. Schaefer. Tucson, The University of Arizona Press.

1994 *Entrada: The Legacy of Spain and Mexico in the United States*. Tucson, Southwest Parks and Monuments Association; Albuquerque, University of New Mexico Press.

Forbes, Robert H.
1952 *Crabb's Filibustering Expedition into Sonora, 1857*. Tucson, Arizona Silhouettes.

Garcés, Francisco
1900 *On the Trail of a Spanish Pioneer. The Diary and Itinerary of Francisco Garcés*. Two volumes. Translated, edited, and annotated by Elliott Coues. New York, Francis P. Harper.

1965 *A Record of Travels in Arizona and California, 1775–1776*. Edited by John Galvin. San Francisco, John Howell —Books.

González R., Luis
1977 *Etnología y misión en la Pimería Alta, 1715–1740*. México, Universidad Nacional Autónoma de México.

Goss, Robert C.
1975 The churches of San Xavier, Arizona and Caborca, Sonora: A Comparative Analysis. *The Kiva*, Vol. 40, no. 3 (Spring), pp. 165–179. Tucson, Arizona Archaeological and Historical Society.

Griffith, James S.
1988 *Southern Arizona Folk Arts*. Tucson, The University of Arizona Press.

1992 *Beliefs and Holy Places: A Spiritual Geography of the Pimería Alta*. Tucson, The University of Arizona Press.

1995 *A Shared Place: Folklife in the Arizona-Sonora Borderlands*. Logan, Utah State University Press.

Herring, Patricia
1978 The Silver of El Real de Arizonac. *Arizona and the West*, Vol. 20, no. 3 (Autumn), pp. 245–258. Tucson, The University of Arizona Press.

Kelemen, Pál
1977 *Vanishing Art of the Americas*. New York, Walker and Company.

Kelly, Sean and Rosemary Rogers
1993 *Saints Preserve Us!* New York, Random House.

Kessell, John L.
1970 *Mission of Sorrows: Jesuit Guevavi and the Pimas, 1691–1767*. Tucson, The University of Arizona Press.

1976 *Friars, Soldiers, and Reformers. Hispanic Arizona and the Sonora Mission Frontier, 1767–1856*. Tucson, The University of Arizona Press.

Kino, Eusebio Francisco
1948 *Kino's Historical Memoir of Pimería Alta*. Two volumes in one. Translated, edited, and annotated by Herbert E. Bolton. Berkeley and Los Angeles, University of California Press.

1971 *Kino's Biography of Francisco Javier Saeta, S.J.* [*Sources and Studies for the History of the Americas*, Vol. 9]. Translated, with an epilogue by Charles W. Polzer; edited by Ernest J. Burrus. Rome, Italy, and St. Louis, Missouri, Jesuit Historical Institute.

Kirk, Ruth
1973 *Desert. The American Southwest*. Boston, Houghton Mifflin Co.

Kissell, Mary L.
1972 *Basketry of the Papago and Pima Indians*. Glorieta, New Mexico, Rio Grande Press, Inc. Reprint of the 1916 Edition.

Krutch, Joseph Wood
1954 *Voice of the Desert*. New York, William Sloan Associates.

1973 *The Desert Year*. New York, Viking Press.

Liberós, Ramón
1822 [Letter dated September 6.] Bancroft Mexican Manuscripts, MM 379, no. 75. Bancroft Library, University of California, Berkeley.

1823 [Letters dated February 3, August 24, and August 27.] Bancroft Mexican Manuscripts, MM 379, nos. 82, 104, and 105. Bancroft Library, University of California, Berkeley.

Lumholtz, Carl
1990   *New Trails in Mexico*. New edition. Tucson, The University of Arizona Press.

Manje, Juan Mateo
1954   *Luz de Tierra Incógnita. Unknown Arizona and Sonora, 1693–1701*. Translated by Harry J. Karns. Tucson, Arizona Silhouettes.

McCarty, Kieran R.
1973   "Franciscan Beginnings on the Arizona-Sonora Desert, 1776–1770." Ph.D. dissertation, The Catholic University of America, Washington, D.C.

1981   *A Spanish Frontier in the Enlightened Age. Franciscan Beginnings in Sonora and Arizona*. [*Monograph Series*, Vol. 13.] Washington, D.C., Academy of American Franciscan History.

McCarty, Kieran R., *translator* and *editor*
1987   Mission manifesto: a document. *The Americas*, Vol. 43, no. 3 (January), pp. 347–354. West Bethesda, Maryland, Academy of American Franciscan History.

Morgan, Richard J., Jr.
1995   *A Guide to Historic Missions and Churches of the Arizona–Sonora Borderlands*. Tucson, Adventures in Education, Inc.

Moyano, Francisco
1803   Noticia de las Misiones, Sonora, Pimería Alta, 1802. Archivo General de Indias, México, Legajo 2736.

1807   Report of January 5. Item no. 2368, Archivo Franciscano, National Library of Mexico, Mexico City. [See Ignacio del Río, *Guía del Archivo Franciscano* (Mexico City and Washington, D.C.) Instituto de Investigaciones Bibliográficas, Universidad Nacional Autónoma, and Academy of American Franciscan History, 1975).]

Nabhan, Gary
1982   *The Desert Smells Like Rain. A Naturalist in Papago Indian Country*. San Francisco, North Point Press.

1985   *Gathering the Desert*. Tucson, The University of Arizona Press.

Nabhan, Gary P., Wendy Hodgson, and Frances Fellows
1990   A Meager Living on Lava and Sand? Hia Ced O'odham Food Resources and Habitat Diversity in Oral and Documentary History. *Journal of the Southwest*, Vol. 31, no. 4 (Winter), pp. 508–533.

Tucson, University of Arizona Press and the Southwest Center.

Naylor, Thomas H., and Charles W. Polzer, *compilers* and *editors*
1988   *Pedro de Rivera and the Military Regulations for Northern New Spain, 1724–1729*. Tucson, The University of Arizona Press.

Nentvig, Juan
1980   *Rudo Ensayo. A Description of Sonora and Arizona in 1764*. Translated and annotated by Alberto Pradeau and Robert R. Rasmussen. Tucson, The University of Arizona Press.

Noticias de las Misiones. Sonora 1803–1804. Archivo Franciscano 37/829. Yarza inventory no. 12 of the Archivo de Indias. Mexico. Legajo 2736.

Officer, James E.
1984   "Cocóspera Valley." Unpublished manuscript. 2 pp. Copy on file with Bernard L. Fontana, Tucson.

1987   *Hispanic Arizona, 1536–1856*. Tucson, The University of Arizona Press.

1991   Mining in Hispanic Arizona: Myth and Reality. In *History of Mining in Arizona*, Vol. 2. Edited by J. Michael Canty and Michael N. Greeley, pp. 1–26. Tucson, Mining Club of the Southwest Foundation and the American Institute of Mining Engineers.

1993   Kino and Agriculture in the Pimería Alta. *The Journal of Arizona History*, Vol. 34, no. 3 (Autumn), pp. 287–306. Tucson, Arizona Historical Society.

Olin, George
1994   *House in the Sun: A Natural History of the Sonoran Desert*. Second edition. Tucson, Southwest Parks and Monuments Association.

Ortiz, Alfonso, *editor*
1983   *Handbook of North American Indians*. Vol. 10 (Southwest), edited by William C. Sturtevant. Washington, Smithsonian Institution. [See the essays on Pima and Papago Indians (pp. 125–216) by Bernard L. Fontana, Paul H. Ezell, Robert A. Hackenberg, Donald M. Bahr, Madeline Mathiot, and Sally Giff Pablo.]

Padrones de las ocho misiones que en la Pimería Alta son a cargo del Colegio Ap.co de la Sta. Cruz de Querétaro. Padrón de la Misión de Propaganda Fide de Sn Joseph de

Tumacácori: Año do 1801. Archivo de la Mitra de Sonora, Hermosillo, Sonora. Roll 28, exposure 5 et seq, Film 422, reel 2, The University of Arizona Library, Tucson.

Parish Archives of Sonora and Sinaloa. Baptisms and Burials. Film 811. Arizpe reels 11 and 12. The University of Arizona Library, Tucson.

Pfefferkorn, Ignaz
1989   *Sonora: A Description of the Province.* Translated by Theodore E. Treutlein. Reprint, with a new introduction by Bernard L. Fontana. Tucson, The University of Arizona Press.

Pickens, Buford, *editor*
1993   *The Missions of Northern Sonora: A 1935 Field Documentation.* Photographs by George Alexander Grant. Tucson, The University of Arizona Press.

Polzer, Charles W.
1972   The Franciscan Entrada into Sonora, 1645–1652. *Arizona and the West,* Vol. 14, no. 3 (Autumn), pp. 253–278. Tucson, The University of Arizona Press.
1976   *Rules and Precepts of the Jesuit Missions of Northwestern New Spain.* Tucson, the University of Arizona Press.
1982   *Kino Guide II: His Missions—His Monuments.* Tucson, Southwestern Mission Research Center, Inc..

Reff, Daniel T.
1991   *Disease, Depopulation, and Culture Change in Northwestern New Spain, 1518–1764.* Salt Lake City, University of Utah Press.

Reyes, Antonio María de los
1772   "Reyes Report of 1772." Translated, with a biographical sketch by Kieran R. McCarty. Unpublished manuscript, Special Collections, The University of Arizona Library, Tucson.

Robinson, William J.
1963   Excavations at San Xavier del Bac, 1958. *The Kiva,* Vol. 29, no. 2 (December), pp. 35–57. Tucson, Arizona Archaeological and Historical Society.
1976   Mission Guevavi: Excavations in the Convento. *The Kiva,* Vol. 42, no. 2 (Winter), pp. 135–175. Tucson, Arizona Archaeological and Historical Society.

Roca, Paul M.
1967   *Paths of the Padres through Sonora. An Illustrated History & Guide to Its Spanish Churches.* Tucson, Arizona Pioneers' Historical Society.

Ronstadt, Edward F., *editor*
1993   *Borderman: The Memoirs of José María Federico Ronstadt.* Albuquerque, University of New Mexico Press.

Ruibal Corella, Juan Antonio
1976   *¡Y Caborca se Cubrió de Gloria . . . ! La expedición filibustera de Henry Alexander Crabb a Sonora.* México, Editorial Porrúa, S.A.

Ruiz, Juanita
1965   Farewell Batuc—a Lost Historic Site. *The Journal of Arizona History,* Vol. 6, no. 3 (Autumn), pp. 152–154. Tucson, Arizona Pioneers' Historical Society.

Salmón, Roberto Mario, *translator,* and Thomas H. Naylor, *editor*
1983   A 1791 report on the Villa de Arizpe. *The Journal of Arizona History,* Vol. 24, no. 1 (Spring), pp. 13–28. Tucson, Arizona Historical Society.

Schaefer, John P.; Celestine Chinn, and Kieran R. McCarty
1977   *Bac: Where the Waters Gather.* [Tucson], privately printed.

Schroeder, Albert H.
1956   Southwestern Chronicle: The Cipias and Ypotlapiguas. *Arizona Quarterly,* Vol. 12, no. 2 (Summer), pp. 101–110. Tucson, University of Arizona.

Schuetz–Miller, Mardith
1993   Architecture. The Spanish Borderlands. In *Encyclopedia of the North American Colonies,* Vol. 3, pp. 286–299. New York, Charles Scribner's Sons.
1994   *Building and Builders in Hispanic California, 1769–1850.* Tucson, Southwestern Mission Research Center, Inc., and Santa Barbara, California, Santa Barbara Trust for Historic Preservation.

Sedelmayr, Jacobo
1747   [Letter to Juan Antonio Balthasar, written from Tubutama, March 22.] Copy in Special Collections, The University of Arizona Library, Tucson.
1751   "Visitation of This New Province of Pimería Alta, 1751." [English translation by Daniel S. Matson.] Copy of Spanish holograph text in Special Collections, The University of Arizona Library, Tucson.

Sheridan, Thomas
1988   Kino's Unforeseen Legacy: The Material Consequences of Missionization among the Northern Piman Indians of Arizona and Sonora. *The Smoke Signal,* nos. 49 and 50 (Spring and Fall), pp. 149, 151–167. Tucson, Tucson Corral of the Westerners.

Shreve, Forrest, and Ira L. Wiggins
1964   *Vegetation and Flora of the Sonoran Desert.* Two volumes. Palo Alto, California, Stanford University Press.

Smith, Fay Jackson
1993   *Captain of the Phantom Presidio: A History of the Presidio of Fronteras, Sonora, New Spain, 1686–1735.* Spokane, Washington, The Arthur H. Clark Company.

Spicer, Edward H.
1962   *Cycles of Conquest: The Impact of Spain, Mexico, and the United States on the Indians of the Southwest, 1533–1960.* Tucson, The University of Arizona Press.

Stagg, Albert
1976   *The First Bishop of Sonora: Antonio de los Reyes, O.F.M.* Tucson, The University of Arizona Press.

Stern, Peter, and Robert Jackson
1988   Vagabundaje and Settlement Patterns in Colonial Northern Sonora. *The Americas*, Vol. 44, no. 4 (April), pp. 461–481. West Bethesda, Maryland, Academy of American Franciscan History.

Stoner, Victor R.
1937   "Original Sites of the Spanish Missions of the Santa Cruz Valley." Unpublished Master's thesis, University of Arizona, Tucson.

Thurston, Herbert, and Donald Attwater, *editors*
1956   *Butler's Lives of the Saints.* Complete edition. Four volumes. New York, P.J. Kenedy and Sons.

Wasley, William W.
1976   Cronología preliminar para las misiones del Padre Kino: Nuestra Señora de los Remedios y Nuestra Señora del Pilar y Santiago de Cocóspera. Traducido por Arturo Olivares M. *Cuadernos de los Centros*, no. 21, part II. Mexico City, Dirección de Centros Regionales, Centro Regional del Noroeste, Instituto Nacional de Antropología e Historia.

West, Robert C.
1993   *Sonora: Its Geographical Personality.* Austin, University of Texas Press.

Williams, Jack
1986a   The Presidio of Santa Cruz de Terrenate: A Forgotten Fortress of Southern Arizona. *The Smoke Signal*, nos. 47–48 (Spring and Fall), pp. 109, 129–148. Tucson, Tucson Corral of the Westerners.
1986b   San Agustín del Tucson: A Vanished Mission Community of the Pimería Alta. *The Smoke Signal*, nos. 47–48 (Spring and Fall), pp. 109, 112–128. Tucson, Tucson Corral of the Westerners.

Wyllys, Rufus K.
1932   *The French in Sonora (1850–1854).* [*University of California Publications in History*, Vol. 21.] Berkeley, University of California Press.

Yturralde, Francisco
1797   "Visita de las misiones de la Pimería Alta, Sept. 5–Oct. 30, 1797." Archivo del Colegio de la Santa Cruz de Querétaro, Celaya, Guanjuato, México. Photocopy and English translation on file with Bernard L. Fontana.

CONTRIBUTORS

Bernard L. Fontana earned his doctorate in anthropology from the University of Arizona. Books by him include *Of Earth and Little Rain: The Papago Indians* (Tucson: The University of Arizona Press, 1989), with photographs by John P. Schaefer, and *Entrada: The Legacy of Spain & Mexico in the United States* (Tucson: Southwest Parks and Monuments Association, 1994). He is retired as Field Historian in the University of Arizona Library.

James S. Griffith's doctorate in anthropology is from the University of Arizona. His many publications include *Beliefs and Holy Places: A Spiritual Geography of the Pimería Alta* (Tucson: The University of Arizona Press, 1992) and *A Shared Space: Folklife in the Arizona-Sonora Borderlands* (Logan: Utah State University Press, 1995). He is director of the Southwest Folklore Center in the University of Arizona Library.

Kieran R. McCarty a Franciscan priest whose doctorate in history is from the Catholic University of America in Washington, D.C., is a research specialist in the Mexican-American Studies Program at the University of Arizona. His publications include *Desert Documentary: The Spanish Years, 1767–1821* (Tucson: Arizona Historical Society, 1976) and *A Spanish Frontier in the Enlightened Age: Franciscan Beginnings in Sonora and Arizona, 1767–1770* (Washington, D.C.: Academy of American Franciscan History, 1981).

James E. Officer earned his doctorate in anthropology from the University of Arizona. The editor of *Anthropology and the American Indian* (San Francisco: The Indian Historian Press, 1973), his magnum opus is *Hispanic Arizona, 1536–1856* (Tucson: The University of Arizona Press, 1987). He was professor emeritus at the University of Arizona.

Mardith Schuetz–Miller received her doctoral degree in American Studies from the University of Texas at Austin. Among her numerous publications are *Building and Builders in Hispanic California, 1769–1850* (Tucson and Santa Barbara: Southwestern Mission Research Center, Inc., and the Santa Barbara Trust for Historic Preservation, 1994) and her edited and annotated translation of *Architectural Practice in Mexico City: A Manual for Journeyman Architects of the Eighteenth Century* (Tucson: The University of Arizona Press, 1987). She is an independent scholar.

Thomas E. Sheridan received his doctoral degree in anthropology from the University of Arizona. His books include *Los Tucsonenses: The Mexican Community in Tucson, 1854–1941* (Tucson: The University of Arizona Press, 1986) and *Arizona: A History* (Tucson: The University of Arizona Press, 1995). He is an ethnohistorian in the Arizona State Museum.

Roberta Stabel is a former naturalist with the National Park Service who was employed at Saguaro National Monument, now Saguaro National Park, in southern Arizona. She presently lives in Tubac, Arizona, where she heads her own real estate business.

Carmen Villa de Prezelski is a native of Tucson and weekly columnist for the *Tucson Citizen* newspaper. Formerly program coordinator for the Southwest Studies Center at the University of Arizona, she is now Assistant to the Director of the university's U.S.-Mexico Educational Interchange Project.